MAPPING THE HEART:
Reflections on Place and Poetry

BOOKS BY WESLEY MCNAIR

POETRY
The Faces of Americans in 1853
The Town of No
My Brother Running
Talking in the Dark
Fire

LIMITED EDITIONS
Twelve Journeys in Maine
The Dissonant Heart

EDITED ANTHOLOGY
The Quotable Moose: Contemporary Maine Writing

MAPPING THE HEART:
Reflections on Place and Poetry

by
Wesley McNair

Carnegie Mellon University Press
Pittsburgh 2003

Acknowledgments

Thanks to the editors of the following magazines, where these essays were originally published, sometimes in different form: *Chelsea, Maine in Print* (in two versions): "Advice for Beginning Poets"; *Chrysalis*: "My Finite Eyes"; *The Green Mountains Review*: "Talking about Vermont: Hayden Carruth's Poetic Voice"; *The Harvard Review*: "The Triumph of Robert Francis"; *The Iowa Review*: "A Government of Two"; *Maine Times*: "The Forest and the Trees," "Letters from a Poet"; *Ploughshares* and *Ploughshares* selections online: "Notes on Poets, Poets Teaching, and Poetry"; *The Sewanee Review*: "Discovering Emily Dickinson," "Places in the Dark," "Placing Myself," "Robert Frost and Dramatic Speech," "Taking the World for Granite: Four Poets in New Hampshire."

Thanks also to the editors of the following anthologies: *In a Hungry Season* (CavanKerry Press) for "John Haines and Vocation"; *Night Errands: How Poets Use Dreams* (University of Pittsburgh Press) for "Dark Deams, Dark Sayings"; and *Telling the Barn Swallow: Poets on the Poetry of Maxine Kumin* (University Press of New England) for an extended essay from which the Kumin segment of "Taking the World for Granite" is derived.

I am grateful to these early readers: Robert Begiebing, Michael Burke, Malcolm Cochran, Daniel Gunn, Donald Hall, Robert Kimber, Diane McNair, Paul McNair, Mike Pride, and Bill Roorbach. For help with manuscript preparation, I am indebted to Jesse Edwards, Dorothy Egan, Douglas Rooks, Catherine Russell, David Scribner and Jean Scribner. For its support of this book project and me as a writer, special thanks to the University of Maine at Farmington.

Publication of this book is supported by a grant from the Pennsylvania Council on the Arts.

Library of Congress Control Number: 20022101899
ISBN: 0–88748–380–1
Printed and bound in the United States of America
Book design and composition by Richard Foerster

10 9 8 7 6 5 4 3

Table of Contents

V. END NOTES

For Diane

I.
Placing Myself

Placing Myself

My older brother writes me from Alabama that if I could taste a fig grown in his garden, I would realize I am living in the wrong location. He may be right. Being the sort of fellow who is often out of place—mistaking the hour, the calendar, or the map—I could easily have gotten the place where I live wrong, too. Yet at age 58, with northern New England in my blood, and in my poems, which amounts to the same thing, I no longer have a choice. I'm here. Figs may not grow in this place, but it is by now pretty clear the place has grown me.

Since I was born in northern New England—Newport, New Hampshire, to be exact—the region is in my earliest memories. Among seasons, I remember winter most—the long, quiet snowfalls, the chinking of tire chains on cars as they passed through the neighborhood, the bleak sunsets that tinted the snow before the onset of darkness. I spent much of my childhood in a low-rent project outside of Springfield, Vermont, called Southview. It was there my father moved us just before he left my mother, my two brothers, and me. His departure filled my days with loneliness and longing; I see as I write this that wherever those feelings may exist in my poems about northern New England, they began that early. One winter morning after he left—did I experience or dream this?—I peered into a deep patch of ice, where I had discovered a large coin attached to a silver key. Frozen there, the coin promised to anyone who could retrieve the key a cash prize of many zeros. With no way to reach what glittered under my hand, I went on looking into the ice, caught in its spell just as the coin and its key were.

In those sunsets of my childhood, I found more longing. Bleak in winter and wistful in summer, they took the world of our play with them and left me and my childhood friends in twilight, listening to the plaintive vowels of our names as our mothers called us home. Do today's children of my region still gather on hills after school in January to see whose sled is the fastest, or play "kick the can" in the long evenings of June? In the 1940s, long before cable TV, the kids of Southview were outdoors as long as light permitted. During the summer, on the hottest days, the assistant manager of the project, a good-hearted man named "Stocker," fit as many of us as he could on the hand-sawed bed of his truck and took us to a nearby lake. I still recall the joy and fear we felt each time that old truck hit a bump dipping us on soft shocks down to the tires; and I can smell the sweet odor of wood against rubber as we went on to the next bump, clinging to one another and shrieking.

In these first years as a New Englander, what do I remember of poetry? I must have written some in elementary school, since I was sometimes called class poet. One day when I was in second grade, my teacher brought a guest to class and passed out a poem in purple ink called "Lilacs," by Robert Frost. Unlikely as it seems by hindsight, she asked the class, not yet finished with the basic reader, to read this poem for discussion, and I had the feeling my response was the one she wanted most. Yet try as I might to understand it, the poem remained impenetrable, and when she called on me, I had nothing to say. I couldn't have known then that this was the beginning of my struggle with Frost, a literary father of sorts, and that one day I would have to find my way past him if I were to become a New England poet.

Nor could I have known that through my mother, I was obtaining a sense of character and story I would later use in narrative poems. Before my father left, she read a long series of Thornton Burgess's *Old Mother West Wind* stories to my brothers and me, and later on, to me alone, the stories of a black child named Little Brown Koko, serialized in *Woman's*

Day magazine. My first book was a collection of these stories, cut out and pasted on construction paper.

Other characters I remember from that time came from humorous anecdotes I heard my mother tell her women friends about people who lived around us in the project. There was Marguerite Coates, who vastly outweighed her little husband Wilmer, and ran him ragged with chores and ultimatums. Since the Coateses lived in the tenement next to ours, we often heard her demands right through the partition, and my mother repeated them, doing her best impression of Mrs. Coates. On the other side of us were the Quelches—Bob and his wife Eleanor, the world's worst house-cleaner. My mother once heard Eleanor's excited voice through the wall as she discovered in a discarded pile of clothes "my old tan suit!" It is perhaps from my mother I got my tendency to use humor in poetry as a release from tension and sorrow; for happiness did not last long in her house. Left by her feckless husband to support three children, she was often upset and angry with us all. I may have gotten certain methods of narration from my mother as well. I have never forgotten the way she told a story, aiming all details at an emotional climax, as I myself try to do. Nor have I forgotten how, switch in hand, she expressed her anger—the mixture of desperation and fear I heard in her voice as it broke through conventional grammar with an emotional syntax of its own. Whenever I write a dramatic monologue involving a speaker under stress, the poem imitates my mother's voice—its thickness of emotion, its sense of language driven by feeling.

It could not have helped my mother's emotional state that ours was one of the poorest families in the project, barely saved from destitution by the sewing she was able to take in and the haircuts she gave neighborhood kids on Saturdays. As I look back on our life then, I recall only a few details of our deprivation: carrying leftovers home from the school cafeteria; standing in front of a small electric heater one day when the coal ran out; wishing for a bicycle my mother could not afford. Yet when I look at the characters who inhabit my poems, it is clear my upbringing has left its mark. Where a poet like Robert Lowell features a New England family of pedigree, connected to the history of high culture in the region, my poetry family is lower class, consisting of mongrels whose history is mostly unknown. Where Donald Hall skips a generation to write about his grandfather and the agrarian tradition he represents, I write about a broken family with no patriarch and no clear tradition. My extra-family characters seem to be marked by my experience in Southview, too; for they are often underprivileged or misfits, living outside the social mainstream.

My life in Southview ended in the summer before I entered fifth grade. That was when my mother remarried, and the new family moved to my stepfather's city of Claremont, New Hampshire, on the other side of the Connecticut River. While we lived in an apartment there and he worked in a machine shop, we helped him settle on land he had purchased in the river valley.

The relationship my brothers and I had with my stepfather was not without conflict. Yet, to see things his way, what was he to do? A relatively simple man, he had in his view provided us with room and board and did not understand why we shouldn't spend our time helping him build a house on his property and raise vegetables and goats there. His response when we were reluctant or broke his rules was harsh, spoiling any chance of a bond with him. But it was my stepfather who introduced me to the farm life that had gone on by the Connecticut for centuries. Eventually, I began to work on other farms in the area, gathering experiences that would one day lead to my own agrarian poems.

The most important experiences came from the Kuhre farm in Cornish, New Hampshire, where I worked in the summer of my fifteenth year. Though I had been accepted for admission at Boys' State, my parents insisted that I take the job in Cornish instead. I was not pleased with the arrangement—particularly when I met the farm's owner, an ancient Danish man who was crippled by a stroke and missing one eye. But the day came when my stepfather dropped me off there, and I entered a world of farming rituals that had been brought from the Old Country, rising with Kuhre's son, a married man who lived upstairs in the farmhouse, to milk the cows, then spending the long day gathering hay and silage.

Poets sometimes speak of making poems from events that linger in the mind waiting to be lived more deeply. Though I did not especially like the work at Kuhre farm, my days were full of such events: the dreamlike movement of the cows as they went out into the field in the morning; tramping on silage as it rained down inside the silo in a green light; the figure of old Kuhre himself on his tractor, circling, as I put it in a later poem, "all my afternoons." Each day after breakfast it was my job to start Kuhre's tractor, one of the first the John Deere company ever made, by turning its immense flywheel again and again. In the meantime, Kuhre would be making his way toward me on a crutch which he then hooked onto the gearshift, hoisting himself into his seat and driving away. At night, the son upstairs with his wife and young boy, Kuhre and his wife sat with me over a late supper of leftovers from the large noon meal. Shipped to New Hampshire from Denmark in an arranged marriage, Mrs. Kuhre had apparently gotten no closer to the old man than I or anyone else had, for she spent the whole meal talking to him in Danish and getting no response except for an occasional grunt. Sitting on his left in that room lit only by a table lamp, I saw an eyeless face when I looked at him, and that view made me feel his silence even more strongly. In a way his alien quality was like the farm itself, an unacculturated place, the more mysterious because the farm life there was so pure. It did not rely, as my stepfather's did, on work elsewhere to support it. Furthermore, it was totally removed from the culture of the megalopolis that had long since arrived in Claremont, through products like margarine and hula-hoops and the rock 'n' roll music I listened to after supper at the farm on the portable radio I kept in my room.

How delicious the voices of Fats Domino, Elvis Presley, and Buddy Holly seemed to me as I brought them in, like contraband, from WBZ, in Boston, or WPTR in Albany, New York. How I looked forward to those moments when, riding a truckload of hay back to the barn, I could pull out the flat piece of wood I carried in my back pocket and strum it while singing my own rock 'n' roll tunes. Putting the ten dollars a week I made at the Kuhre farm away, I was saving my money for an electric guitar and amplifier; in the meantime, I learned chords by playing this soundless instrument, on which I had drawn fret lines and tacked string. Later on, in college, I would play in a rock band, using the guitar I finally purchased with my summer earnings. Still later, when I no longer played, I would express my love of American popular culture through images of comic book thugs, hair on television, and big cars—then write long pieces that mixed the popular and rural cultures together. Edward Hopper once maintained that no artist ever changes much, only refines the tendencies with which he began. As a poet in my middle fifties, I may well be back where I was at 15: part of me in the farmhouse, the other part in the culture of Everywhere, U.S.A.

Eventually, the Kuhre farm dissolved. A decade after I stopped working there, the old man was run over by his tractor in a freak accident, and his son, who had acquired two hernias and expenses he could not meet, gave up farming. By that time it was clear to me the Kuhre farm had all along been an anomaly in a region where the old ways of agriculture had been disintegrating for years, and farmhouses on large acreages were being replaced by ranch-style houses on small parcels of land like my parents'. But while my work at Kuhre farm during that summer and later school vacations lasted, I learned farming's old ways. In addition I heard stories from Kuhre's son and an aging hired hand named Rick about rural characters: the alcoholic farmer who attached a spigot to the bottom of his silo to bottle fermented corn juice, or the lazy neighbor who sometimes let his cows go unmilked until they bawled for mercy. The jokes they told were often an established part of the work ritual, the teller taking pleasure from having remembered them for the correct occasion. So when I or a local boy hired part time for haying tossed a bale onto the wrong part of the load, Rick would invariably shout down: "Aim for the sun, shoot at the moon, and don't hit either one." And so each time we unloaded the truck in the hay mow, someone would remark to the person who lifted the final bale, "That's the one we've been looking for—why didn't you send it up in the first place?"

New Hampshire contributed in one more way to my development as a poet when I got a job the next summer at Lost River Gorge in the White Mountains. A kitchen boy, I was making twenty-two dollars a week, more than double the salary I had made at the Kuhre farm. Moreover, I got the chance to meet and talk with the college students who led tours through the gorge. In this way I met John, a literature student at Columbia University, with a passion for poetry. The poems we shared and the discussions we had about them resulted in one of the most important pieces of mail I ever received: a small, heavy box that arrived the next spring, bearing my name in bold letters. At the time, John must have been moving out of his dorm room, since the box was packed with books he had purchased for college courses or for recreational reading during the school year. There were novels by William Faulkner, Carson McCullers, and Ernest Hemingway; collections of essays by Randall Jarrell and R. P. Blackmur on the work of Cummings, Moore, Frost, and others; and poetry by Cummings, Williams, Ferlinghetti, and the pre-*Waste Land* Eliot. Having such volumes to read as a high school student in the boondocks of western New Hampshire gave me a feeling for the modern tradition in America that might otherwise have taken me years to acquire. And finding a copy of Columbia University's literary magazine with a poem by John himself in it suggested to me that I might one day be able to publish my own poetry.

Still, it would be years before I completed my first poems about the rural life I had discovered in the Connecticut River Valley. I married in my last college year, and because my wife brought two children to the marriage and both of us were working, I had little time for a writing career, and even less time in the years that followed, when we had two more children and I started a graduate degree. It wasn't only the lack of time, however, that prevented me from writing poems. I was disenchanted with poetry, having become convinced that poetry was supposed to be difficult. As an undergraduate at Keene State College hoping to become a poet, I had heard an aging Ramon Guthrie, then in his last years of teaching at Dartmouth, read poems freighted with mythological and cultural references, and I had learned from my English teachers about the importance of T. S. Eliot's *Waste Land*—a poem I respected but had trouble understanding, as I had trouble with the obscure verse of New Critical poets I found at the college library in back issues of *Poetry*. True, I had come to know the much more accessible Lawrence Ferlinghetti through the box John sent me; I was aware of Gregory Corso and Allen Ginsberg as well. Yet while Eliot and the New Critics seemed too cerebral and complex, much of Beat poetry seemed too simple, and its subject matter too involved with the West Coast. For his part Robert Frost, whose poetry I had read and explored extensively in the years since my first encounter with him in second grade, seemed old-fashioned.

My solution was to put poetry aside, I thought for good, and spend the few hours I had for writing on short stories. I have read that as a young writer E. A. Robinson was able to sidestep the sentimental verse of his time and develop his narrative techniques by turning away from poetry for a time ("the enemy," he called it) and working on prose sketches. As it turned out, my efforts on stories helped me in the same way, allowing me to find an alternative to both New Critical and Beat poetry in my own narrative poems. While I was writing fiction, I was also trying to draw cartoons, and they, too, had their influence on my poetry—not only because they helped bring cartoons and pop visuals into my verse as a subject, but because the single-caption cartoon I was attempting is so much like the lyrical narrative of my later verse: One places two or three characters together in a certain resonant situation, touches just the right words against them, and poof! the cartoon comes to life. The narrative poem is less static than the single-caption cartoon, of course, but there is a similar interest in the moment, and in the compression and tone of language. For years I tried unsuccessfully to publish the stories or the cartoons I worked on, regularly cursing my luck. Now I see there was luck in the venture after all.

I wrote my first narrative poem as an adult at Lake Mascoma in Enfield, New Hampshire, when I was twenty-eight years old. At the time, my family and I had just been turned out of a lovely old cape we had rented for five years, near Newport and not far from my job at Colby Junior—later, Colby-Sawyer—College. Though my wife was pregnant with a fourth child, the family that owned the house pressured us to leave after only a month's notice, then showed up on moving day to urge us out and cut down two of our favorite trees. Not knowing what else to do, we prevailed upon my in-laws to let us stay at their cottage on the lake until we could go elsewhere. There, I put aside the short stories I had been working on to begin "Leaving the Country House to the Landlord," a poem about our traumatic move.

The necessity of this poem, which forced me back to poetry, also compelled me to make use of approaches I had learned as a fiction writer. Stanza by stanza, I composed a series of scenes or moments that revealed the one family packing up and moving out, and the other family cutting down trees and moving in. The difference between my poem and the fiction I had worked on was that in the poem, all of the scenes took place simultaneously in one spot of time. Impatient always with the linear requirements of plot in the short story—that "and then, and then-ness"—I was able at last to tell a story that seemed to take place all at once, combining elements of narration with a sense of the lyric. Having learned this lesson, which influenced all the poems I wrote afterward, I never returned to fiction.

People who lived through the assassination of President Kennedy remember where they were when they got the news; I recall exactly where I was when I learned that my first poem had been accepted for publication. Standing outside of the post office in Enfield near the end of my family's fateful summer, I had just picked up the mail that had collected there for two or three weeks. By then, my family and I were living in the home of my in-laws in Keene so they could have the cottage for the month of August. Too broke even to have our car aligned, I had driven for weeks to a summer job on badly scalloped front tires. In short, things couldn't have been worse—until I opened my letter of acceptance from *Poetry Northwest*. The steering wheel shaking in my hands, I drove all the way to Keene weeping and shouting, "I've found a form!" Though I now find a certain awkwardness in the poem that once rescued me from my formless life, the moment when I arrived in Keene to share my good fortune with my wife Diane is still vivid and perfect in my mind.

I realize now that when I finally worked on my poem about the Kuhre farm, "Memory of Kuhre," I made use of what "Leaving the Country House" taught me about the simultaneous story, deploying a series of small events to create the illusion, if not quite the reality, of a single day moving into the next. I wrote the poem after I learned of Kuhre's death, and while he often appears in it, silent and eyeless at the supper table, or driving the tractor that killed him, there is a feeling that he cannot be reached. In part this feeling has to do with the death, and is a way of memorializing him. But I think it is also related to my unreachable father, whom I have often written about since, and to the farm that vanished after Kuhre died, itself unreachable now, as in a sense it was when I worked there, with its unacculturated rituals from the Old World, and that old woman, Kuhre's wife, talking on and on in a language I did not understand.

Whatever I knew about the demise of the farming culture in general when I wrote "Memory of Kuhre" was derived in part from my experience on Hominy Pot Road, where my family and I lived for eighteen years following our departure from Newport. I have often thought that it took me all of those eighteen years to understand this road and assimilate it into my poetry. Hominy Pot, which given its usual condition, we sometimes called Hominy Pothole, stretched for three miles from North Sutton, founded in the late 1700s, to the turnpike that led to Boston and the megalopolis, built in the early 1960s. Traveling the road, one saw a history of diminishing farms, their acreage first sold off for vacation retreats along the lake, then for the nine-hole golf course across the road from our property. Among the sellers was a farmer who once lived in our house, a two-apartment tenement by the time we got there. He was an alcoholic, and he took parcels of land to market every time he ran out of money for drink. A half-mile down the road, another farmhouse had been transformed into a real-estate office, selling what its sign called "Country Estates," as if one needed a reminder that the whole territory, including the self-consciously antique houses of an affluent town nearby, was becoming an artifact, the "Olde New England" version of the agrarian life that had been lost. In the period when my family and I resided on Hominy Pot, a relative newcomer was buying up rural buildings in disrepair and hauling them into the yard around his farmhouse where he renovated them to create what he called a "farm museum." One day we saw this man examining the barn across the road that once housed the alcoholic farmer's cows. Later, a crew showed up to take the barn away, piece by piece. We later learned that the local ski resort, which had bought the barn for storage, had sold it to recoup losses from the previous winter.

In spite of all the changes I saw on Hominy Pot Road, there were certain moonlit nights when the golf course off in the mist looked like a newly mowed field, and when the farmhouse with white clapboard gleaming through the trees seemed not to belong to the golf course's owners, but to a farm family that inhabited it years before. Walking the road on such nights, I sometimes felt a longing for what was gone— a longing akin, perhaps, to what I felt in the landscape around me as a child after my father left. I had a sense of elders in general who had disappeared, and of the mysterious lives they must have lived. It may have been that my night strolls drew me more closely to poems by Edwin Arlington Robinson like "Mr Flood's Party," with its estranged elder who walks in the dark, caught between two cultures. I do know that I began to teach that poem and others by Robinson in the years when I was walking or driving down Hominy Pot, and I also began at that time to see the issue of cultural change in the poems of Robert Frost—how, for instance, the two who mend the stone wall in Frost's famous poem live, ironically, on dead farms. Thus the narrator's complaint, "There where it is we do not need the wall:/ He is all pine and I am apple orchard/ . . . here there are no cows."

Writing poems like "The Last Time Shorty Towers Fetched the Cows," I tried to incorporate what my road had taught me. The poem's inspiration was an article in New Hampshire's *Concord Monitor* about a town historian who had discovered the story of a drunk man out shingling a roof one afternoon. At a certain moment, this man abruptly stood up, announced to his fellow workers that he was going to fetch the cows for milking, and walked off the roof. In the historian's account, the man is not hurt by the fall, but the character in my poem, who owns the house he works on, kills himself, giving a feeling of tragedy to what might have been a comic disorientation. Other changes I made in the newspaper's story show the influence of Hominy Pot. The house in question is a farmhouse, and its back pasture, like the one on the road, has been turned into a golf course. The drunk farmer of the historian's account, who initially reminded me of my house's alcoholic farmer, bears the name of a drunk carpenter who had lived a couple of driveways down for a time—a name so right for my poem, I could not resist it. As it happened, the brother-in-law of this carpenter owned the farmhouse and golf course on Hominy Pot Road; he was the brother-in-law I put on the roof with Shorty. Mixing real-life details with the ones in the historian's account, and adding what I imagined, I shaped my poem into a parable of a man who was confused not only by alcohol, but by the changes around him.

Another poem I wrote at this time deals with the dilemma of telling stories about the vanished past and creating history through them—a theme touched on in "Shorty Towers." Called "Mute," the poem is a composite of three different story fragments I heard while living on Hominy Pot Road. Piecing together all of these half-stories, I created my poem's story, which is itself incomplete; so in the process of telling it the narrator asks questions about the missing details. That narrator was me on Hominy Pot road, puzzling over how to account for the lost culture whose vestiges I saw all around me.

I have said that the early years of my marriage interfered with the writing of poetry, but ultimately, my marriage has been lucky for my poems. For one thing, it has given me a wife who is herself a storyteller, finding characters and events in what might seem to be the uninspiring details of a day at work or at home. First hearing how she altered details from one telling to another as she sharpened her narratives, I used to complain, "But that's not how it happened." Eventually, as it became clear that we were in the same business of lying to tell the truth, I began to appreciate the liberties she took, and even learn from them.

Another benefit of my marriage has been my relationship with my wife's mother and aunts and cousins—women who once worked on farms in this region and have occasionally told me their own stories. Their memories, recalled in Yankee accents, of the old days, and their lives themselves, have offered me glimpses of an earlier New England and allowed me to find a deeper connection between the past and the present. Often I have adapted these women or the stories they have told for poems. The Mina Bell of "Mina Bell's Cows," an old farm widow who keeps three pet cows too old for milking, is one of my wife's aunts, or a version of her; this same aunt is the source for the country woman who washes her middle-aged son's hair each week in "Making Things Clean." The tale of the young girl who spies her naked and crazy aunt through the keyhole in her grandparents' farmhouse in the "The Secret" is loosely based on a story my wife's cousin told me at a family reunion. My most valuable informant, however, was my mother-in-law. It was she who told me about pet cows her sister kept, the unusual shampoo her sister gave to her son each washday, and even the deaf mute I wrote about in "Mute." It was also my mother-in-law who mentioned, when my wife and I took her on a tour of her birthplace in Benton, New Hampshire, the strange courtship between another sister and her rural beau, both of whom I wrote about in "Young Man Going Uphill with a Bird." Not a person for details, my mother-in-law provided little more than the framework for a story and sometimes not even that, but there was usually enough in what she told to dream on. It may be true as some have said that the poems she and other relatives inspired contain feelings more tender than those of other poems I have written, or particular insights into the world of femalehood; if so, it is because the poems came from women in the first place.

In the middle of my exploration of Hominy Pot Road, the stories of family relatives, and the poems of New England poets (including Emily Dickinson, by then a staple in my undergraduate course, "Dickinson and Frost") I met Donald Hall and Jane Kenyon, living 10 miles away in Wilmot, New Hampshire. In the years afterward, I became acquainted with Maxine Kumin, located 10 or 12 miles in the other direction, and Charles Simic, who lived 40 miles beyond her. Just knowing Kumin and Simic were nearby made me feel the importance of poetry in my rural world even before I met them. But the relationship I developed with Hall was crucial to me as a poet. We were introduced by two of my former students in the fall of 1976, shortly after Hall had moved into his ancestral home.

At the time, he was beginning the poems about New Hampshire that would be collected in *Kicking the Leaves* (1978), and I was at a crossroad. Just appointed as coordinator of an American studies program and on my way to becoming a Fulbright professor in American literature and culture at the Catholic University of Chile, I felt the pull of scholarship in my area of teaching. Yet poetry was what I loved—so much so that I had begun to have nightmares about the professional life I was drifting into. I needed someone to tell me I was good enough as a poet to pursue what I loved.

That someone was Donald Hall. Reading a chapbook manuscript I had placed on the kitchen table on my way out of his farmhouse after my visit, he wrote to say how much he liked my poems and invited me back again to praise them in person. The impact of his appreciation was enormous, convincing me to put aside scholarly ambitions and even to step down as coordinator of American studies, as I did two years later. Today, twenty years into our friendship, I do not see him often, but we correspond and exchange poems regularly, and I continue to value his opinion of my work.

I do not want to suggest that my scholarship and teaching in American studies were unrelated to my verse, even though I might have said so at the time. I now see that my work in American studies gave me a comprehensive understanding of the culture that helped me to write my later, long poems. Just as important, my classes and lectures on American painting sharpened my awareness of how simultaneous storytelling can be. For all the great American painters are storytellers whose plots are given in a single setting, all at once. Preparing for weekly discussions about the ways in which the landscape artist Thomas Cole portrayed New World nature, or Winslow Homer pitted mariners against the sea, or Edward Hopper related characters to the ironies of light, I was also preparing for my own narratives in poetry.

In the fall of 1987, I moved from Hominy Pot Road to take a job at the University of Maine in Farmington. The most obvious reason was that Colby-Sawyer College—the new name for the college where I started—had fallen on hard times, with diminishing enrollments and low salaries. Another reason was that I had finished my second book of verse, *The Town of No*, and with that volume completed my study of my road and its New England. Taking up residence in Mercer, several miles north of the coastal strip by which outsiders know Maine, I found a New England I hadn't experienced before. For one thing I saw a number of working farms. Furthermore there was less uniformity in the houses around me, and where older houses existed, there was less self-consciousness about their antiquity. As a matter of fact, some of the old houses were decorated with large butterflies, or accompanied by signs reading "Egg's" or "Free Kitten's," with their apostrophes faithfully misplaced. Of course, the late twentieth century had made its impact on my new place as well, and so I passed the same mixture of hay barns and TV dishes on the way to work that I remembered from New Hampshire—where, lest I leave the wrong impression, rural character yet remains, particularly in northern latitudes. After all I once found in New Hampshire the most engaging sign I have seen in northern New England; hanging beside a mailbox on a back road, it announced "Hairdressing and Nightcrawlers." All the same my new location, a little farther than I had been from the humming megalopolis, gave me the impression of a rural culture that slow change had more completely preserved. In its amalgam of the old and the new, not quite either thing, was a lack of acculturation similar, in its way, to what I experienced long before on the old Kuhre farm. Living and writing in Maine, I feel to this day that I am able to discover sides of life that are themselves unacculturated—and find unknown sides of myself.

Discovering the unknown is, in any event, an old theme in Maine, the largest and least settled state in New England. Though it was granted statehood in 1820, large areas were still considered part of the American frontier; even today its map is mostly white space, unmarked by roads. As I once said in my introduction to *The Quotable Moose*, a book of Maine writing, the appeal of a wild territory beyond the reach of civilization brought the first homesteaders to the state from the confinements of life in the Massachusetts Bay Colony, and afterward, in the nineteenth century, inspired a literature and art of exploration. "It is the Montana of New England," I recall remarking to my wife in the enthusiasm of our move, and through poems later collected in a chapbook called *Twelve Journeys in Maine*, I conducted explorations of my own.

Some have found a bleakness in this collection, maybe because it begins with poems that are dark in their settings and subject matter. My own feeling is that the book affirms the country and town life I saw around me. After the first poems, it moves to a benevolent vision through rural settings and characters that are part of an organic tradition, even as they bring together the old and the new, the pure and the impure. One of these characters is Francis in "Francis Bound." Born in my town, he was carried off as an adolescent to California by his hitch in the Navy, returning years later with a California wife and the same, odd Yankee accent he had when he left. The opposite of the town's prevailing dialect—a slow and plaintive pattern of speech whose sentences are inflected sorrowfully upward by habit—Francis' way of speaking is high-speed and a bit frantic, with sentences that get going so fast, they outpace his thought, leaving him stammering and stuttering. In "Francis Bound" Francis never stops talking; the poem's wildly irregular lines are meant to suggest how his talk sounds.

For me, the climax of Maine affirmation in *Twelve Journeys* is the penultimate poem, "Reading Poems at the Grange Meeting in What Must Be Heaven." I wrote it after a woman in my town called me up to explain that "Hobby Night" was taking place at the next Grange meeting, and to ask if I would come and talk about my hobby of writing poetry. Though I was a little reluctant, I went anyway and was won over by the whole event, finding the odd and yet vital mixture I have mentioned everywhere in the Grange hall—from a supper of "burnished/ lasagna squares, thick/ clusters of baked/ beans, cole slaw pink// with beet juice," to the small furniture for the meeting which, donated by the elementary school, made the officers look "as if all three were in fifth grade." The poem's people, too, are a mix, consisting of the old who know the Grange rituals well and others who don't, like Lenny, the trucker, invited to play his spoons, and the two retarded men "pledging allegiance in words/ they themselves have never heard." It is to this diverse group I give my reading in the poem, showing as I do so what sustains my poetry in the new place, and what people my poetry ultimately speaks for. In writing the piece and other poems like it, I am encouraged not so much by Robert Frost as by Walt Whitman.

At the same time I worked on *Twelve Journeys in Maine*, I was writing "My Brother Running," the most necessary poem I have ever done. It is based on the wildly happy and desperate last months of my younger brother's life, which ended with a fatal heart attack. In those months, he jogged relentlessly, sometimes for hours, and his heart attack was related to his running. What made the poem so necessary to write was that he chose me as a confidante in this troubled period, even though we had been estranged for years, telling me alone secrets which, as I put it in the poem, "set him into motion." Then, unpredictedly and abruptly, he died, leaving me with his secrets as well as his problems of the heart—for his heart problems were more than physiological—and leaving me with the memory of his compulsive running.

As a result, though I have never liked long poems, I sat down to begin a long narrative about my brother and our family, trying to discover through it what he was running from, and what he was running to. The problems in making this poem seemed to me almost insurmountable. The first was that though I was compelled to tell the truth about my brother's real life, I had to lie, shaping what really happened into what might or should have happened. It took me a long time to relearn my old trust in poetry and its higher truth. The second problem was how to tell the story so that it would not be linear and prose-like, but instead, like poetry, kaleidoscopic. I finally saw that by coming back to the action of the run again and again and organizing the rest of the poem around it, I could create both the illusion of simultaneity and a sense of emotional urgency. Though composing "My Brother Running" was a much greater challenge than writing "Leaving the Country House to the Landlord" had been, the long poem is, if I am lucky, similar to the shorter one in its effect of "all-at-onceness." So in "My Brother Running" I was finally assisted by lessons in storytelling I had learned from my first poem years earlier.

I wrote a handful of other poems about my family and its difficulties previous to "My Brother Running"; still, I had never dealt so extensively with that theme until then. So it is perhaps natural that reviewers have focused on the domestic and psychological aspects of the poem rather than its commentary about New England. Recently one reviewer even declared that while New England was important to other poems in my book *My Brother Running*, its title poem, had nothing to do with region. In fact I have never been more serious about region as I am in this poem. That is why "My Brother Running" goes beyond local color and folkways to show northern New England in the context of broad historical and social forces. Changing my brother's real-life location, I placed him in Boston, northern New England's biggest city, associating the running he does there among pylons and blown-out strips with the ever-accelerating motion of the megalopolis. New Hampshire in the poem is related to the southern New Hampshire where I grew up and spent my early adult years, a location that urban pressures have dramatically altered. So the mother in the poem tends a failing nursery and truck garden on a plot opposite a commercial garage and just down the turnpike from the K-Mart tree and bush concession. So the brother sets out on his first run in an environment that suggests cultural dissolution, including random trailers, farmhouses, and condos built to look like farmhouses. It is not an accident that the brothers are best able to communicate with each other in central Maine, or that the younger brother has his vision of a home "a million miles from the suburbs" there. In actual fact, all my conversations with my brother during the time of his troubles took place in New Hampshire, not Maine, the state where I moved after he died. But I put the two brothers in my area of Maine anyway because, as I have said, this seems to me a location, not unlike northerly areas of New Hampshire and Vermont, in which change has happened slowly and the rural culture retains a certain integration. Therefore, it seemed an appropriate retreat from the motion and disorientation of the south, a place where the narrator might achieve an understanding of the brother and all that drove him—as I myself did, writing my poem in Maine.

From this place in northern New England where I live in my late middle age, I have been able to see far enough back into my life among the forces of family and history to complete another long poem, and to write two new books of poems, whose universals have roots in the local. It seems to me that such roots have given us some of the best poetry we have in English, from Chaucer to Wordsworth to Yeats, from Whitman to Dickinson to Frost. This fact keeps me reaching beyond whatever gift I may have. Could it be that the dullness and homogeneity of so much contemporary verse results from a rootlessness among our poets, who live in university towns far from their home ground? I am inclined to believe it does. I think of the moral which my long poem "My Brother Running" has taught me: that understanding and vision best come to those who are able to settle down and be still. Sometimes when I myself am still, I think of the boy I was once, discovering the mysterious key in the ice during the winter season he is just beginning to know. Under his hand in the right light, he can make out the attached coin and the prize it guarantees the finder. Even now I can see its long shaft and oval top, wide as the pad of a thumb. For I am that boy, still spellbound by what my place keeps beneath the surface, by the promise of a key.

≈ MAPPING THE HEART ≈

II.
Vocation

John Haines and Vocation

When John Haines came to my campus of the University of Maine in Farmington two years ago to do a reading, I put him up at the same local motel where we lodge all of our visiting writers. Behind the front desk when we walked into the office was the clerk, who gave Haines the keys to his room and a remote for his TV. Haines took his keys, then picked up the remote control and stared at it. "What's this?" he asked. The woman at the desk looked at him, this elderly man with gray hair and glasses who held the remote as if it were a moon rock, seeing him for the first time.

"Why, it's a remote for your TV," she said.

Haines stared some more, until the function of the plastic object in his hand clarified; then he handed it back to her. "I won't be needing *that*," he told her. Now she was the one holding the remote with a baffled expression.

It was comic, this stand off between John Haines and the motel clerk, but serious as well, underscoring the life Haines had lived apart from technology and its dependencies, and taking me back to the poet I discovered long before through early poems and a prose volume called *Living Off the Country*, one of the most significant books I read as a younger writer. Arriving on the American literary scene after years of homesteading in Alaska, years spent developing on his own as a poet, the Haines of that book asked questions about things the poetry establishment had long taken for granted. How was it possible, given the emphasis on careerism and the winning of prizes, for poets to achieve their full maturity? Was the graduate school workshop the best place for a young poet, needing solitude and his own period of gestation? Where were the ideas in contemporary American poetry? And what was one to make of the resemblance between the contemporary poem and the technological device—each a lifeless object, each replaced the next year by another, slightly altered model? Shouldn't a poem be more than a gadget like—well, like the remote for a TV? It is no wonder that John Haines' book, and some of its essays when they originally appeared, caused consternation in an establishment sure, as was the clerk in my local motel, that what it had to offer was what anyone would want to have.

But *Living Off the Country* did not offend me; I identified with it. I had never been to the wilderness of Alaska, but my own location of North Sutton, New Hampshire, often seemed as far outside the poetry loop as his was. My first exposure to the literary scene came in the early 1970's when, as a teacher in the English department at the nearby college in New London, I perused the poetry magazines my office mate had on his shelves—ragged journals with names like *The Small Pond* and *Yes: A Magazine of Poetry*—finding poems that felt willed and incomplete. Once, my office mate lent me a book called *The Young American Poets*. Was it me, or were these poems, too, mostly bad, I wondered. I had nobody, really, to ask, and nobody to tell me later on, when I traveled to the Poetry Room at Dartmouth College, which of the national magazines displayed there might the best outlets for my own poems. As it turned out, I needn't have fussed so much in making my choices. The journals to which I submitted my early poems most often rejected them; worse still, while my office mate turned out poems left and right, my own output was aggravatingly slow. I couldn't seem to find a subject that satisfied me or an approach that would lead me from one poem to the next. The father of a growing family who devoted his summers to graduate school, I had little opportunity for writing, in any case. My notebooks were full of poems I could not finish.

In its commentary about what poems are, the process by which they are created, and the trajectory of the true poet's development, *Living Off the Country* provided a context for my initial struggles as a writer and gave me something to strive for. Most of Haines' readers probably did not notice that just beneath the book's controversy was a set of precepts about the poet's vocation, but I did, and I heard in the voice that enunciated them a rock-like authority that I clung to. Rereading *Living Off the Country* today, I am still struck by that voice— its sense of a speaker saying what he means, and of meaning fastened deep in the page. In every line, there is the feeling of character, and I realize now that this character, evident in all the prose Haines has written since, influenced my attitude toward poetry in my formative years as much as any particular remark he made.

My first reading of *Living Off the Country* began with Haines' review, reprinted from *kayak*, of the book I had seen a short time before, *The Young American Poets*. I still remember how bracing that review was. Preparing to be told I was wrong in my negative assessment of the book, I discovered Haines and I were in agreement. Furthermore, he explained his views about the book's poets in a way that showed me the value of my own struggle with uncertainty, even honored it. The trouble is, he wrote, that few of the poets

> know what a poem is. What is needed for good poems, besides exceptional talent, is patience, and a willingness to live, if necessary, in some solitude and obscurity while one's life and talent mature, even if that takes many years. . . . People instinctively wise know this and do not attempt to force their work into the open before it is ripe. And it is just this solitude that American literary life, with its magazine pages to be filled, its reputations to be made, its prizes to be given, so easily destroys.

I soon learned that the subject of solitude was an important one for this poet who had spent so much time by himself in Alaska. Nearly all of the essays in *Living Off the Country* touched on the subject in some way, and each reference seemed addressed to me alone, especially the passages that linked solitude with place. For like Haines, I myself had written poems about the north— that is, northern New England— and I was increasingly involved with my own place's meaning. "I think, he said in "The Writer as Alaskan,"

> there is a spirit of place, a presence asking to be expressed; and sometimes when we are lucky as writers, and quiet in a way few of us want to be anymore, a voice enters our own, becomes mingled with it, and we speak with a force and clarity not otherwise heard.

This way of speaking through place and for it could only result from a long and observant residence, Haines said, after which the poet might find "another place" inside himself, describing, in the end, all places. As a student of American literature, I was familiar with such ideas; in fact, I had even read the text Haines cited in his essay, D.H. Lawrence's *Studies in Classic American Literature*. But the awareness I had was still an intellectual one. Haines' real-life experience with place helped carry what my head had known into my hands and feet, the American tradition now ready for use.

In "Roots" Haines spoke of a "ferocious transience" that swirled around the poet, making rootedness the more necessary. The essay's model was Robinson Jeffers, a poet who combined his life with his vocation, building his own house on the shoreline of Carmel, California, stone by stone in the same deliberate way he made his poems, with their own hold on place. Without some similar means of "standing aside," Haines warned, poets would only write verse that imitated the quick change and confusion of our technological society. Elsewhere, he spoke about the value of a literary tradition in providing steadiness and constancy. Put aside the fashion of graduate school poems, he implied in his essay "A Hole in the Bucket," recommending that poets learn from past writers how to combine the contemporary with the ancient:

Innovations in style, strange, disordered syntax, unusual images, idiomatic explosions—these soon pass, or are means to an end. Only that remains which touches our deepest, most enduring self. Behind every word is the memory of another, spoken a thousand times; in the intonation of the voice, in the rise and fall of the syllables, memory does its work and reconciles the poet and the reader to a world difficult and strange.

As he had in his description of place's influence on the poet, Haines referred in this passage to a deeper and clearer way of speaking in poetry. Surely no one has expressed more eloquently the value of the literary past to the poet.

In another essay, "Anthologies and Second Thoughts," John Haines wrote a paragraph that still bears the signs of my excited discovery more than fifteen years ago, its words starred and underlined. The paragraph had special value, I see now, because it put into one place all the advice to young poets I had found scattered throughout Haines' book. I quote most of the starred paragraph below.

[Poets]. . . must find ways to be still in themselves, to listen and to silence the noise about and within them. Forget, if you can, about success in the market, ambition, career—all that is merely in the way. Read as much as you can. Read the earth around you, as well as books. Don't be content to imitate your contemporaries and have their approval. Seek out the poets who exemplify the real tradition, one that goes back thousands of years, surviving every disaster. And keep to yourself; don't expect schools to do much for you;lasting poems are not likely to be written in a graduate seminar. Remember that all of our great poets in the past rose by their own efforts out of their own environment.

As meaningful as this advice was to me at a crucial time in my development, I now understand that it is timeless, relevant to young poets or older ones anytime, anywhere.

One of the things I anticipated most about John Haines' visit to my college in Maine two autumns ago was the chance to let him know how much his poems and *Living Off the Country* had meant to me and still meant, all those years later. In fact, this was what I told him shortly after I picked him up from a nearby campus where he'd given a reading the night before, adding my admiration for his new book of essays then just out, *Fables and Distances.* For the rest of our trip, Haines did not, like other visiting poets, talk about the literary scene. He was interested in the place he had come to. How early did it snow? he wanted to know. What kinds of deciduous trees grew here? Where were the state's mountains located? When we arrived in Farmington—on our way to the local motel where Haines would ask still another question, about a TV remote—I stopped in the parking lot outside my campus building, leaving him in the car while I went inside to get a handout of his poems my classes had been studying. To my surprise, he wasn't in the car on my return, or anywhere around it. Then I spotted him exploring a nearby wooded area, exactly where I should have predicted he'd be: by himself, away from the noise of arriving and departing cars, reading the earth.

Discovering Emily Dickinson

One January semester in a basement room at Colby-Sawyer College, the stylish private school for women where I once taught, I discovered Emily Dickinson. Come to think of it, this was the perfect place in that college *to* find her. Who knows whether she even would have shown herself in the conventional classrooms off the upstairs hall, lined with its tasteful wainscoting and gilded portraits? In the room where I held my class, a windowless, catacomb-like place with painted mortar and mismatched desk-chairs, she appeared among us almost every day.

Not every day, because some days I myself did not appear. Once after an an overnight snowstorm, I couldn't get out of my driveway. Another time it was too cold for my car to start. But mainly through the thick of snowdrift and thin of cold patch, that old car got me there. A worn Dodge Coronet station wagon held together by epoxy, the vehicle was like my life itself then. I had four kids in the house, two of them the wildest kind of teenagers; a weary wife, who was working two jobs to make up for the salary I didn't have; pieces of a graduate degree I was trying to put together during summers; and an old dream of becoming a poet that continued to plague me though I had hardly any time to write. What I did with my life was what I did with that station wagon: get in each day, aim it, and hope for the best.

No doubt my situation at the time helped to draw Dickinson out. I don't just mean my personal need for poetry, or my need for guidance from a poet. I mean that odd sense one can have, when all security has been stripped away, of possibility—a feeling, despite despondency, of reassurance that comes from discovering one's true smallness among the forces. Preparing for my classes and only a step or two ahead of my students, I found a poet who valued smallness, often speaking for the smallest among us: bats, rats, toads, hummingbirds, a baby speaking from its grave, a child beggar, nobody. Again and again her message seemed to be, travel light. Riches, want, fame, and social status will make us less aware of the world around us and bog down the spirit besides. I could easily see how good such a message would be for my students, raised in their status-conscious families. I see now how good it was for their impecunious and obscure teacher, who wished himself for some of the things Dickinson warned against.

So when we took off our winter coats each day in that basement room—they, their fashionable ski-jackets and I, my frayed denim one—the ritual was important for all of us. How large those coats, the protective layers that announced who we were to others, seem to me by hindsight, cast aside on empty chairs! What remained was us, the small humans underneath, opening our books together to examine Dickinson's strange code of the feeling life: a collection of short stanzas randomly capitalized and punctuated by dashes.

Breaking the code—one of poetry's principal delights—gave no pleasure to most of my students at first. Chosen from the middle to the lower levels of their high-school classes, they had been left out of the secret language of the classroom before and were not enthusiastic about repeating the experience. But I managed to shake them free from their fears by turning to Dickinson's early letters. There they found a young woman not so different from themselves. For Dickinson, like many of my students, was a teenager sent to a school for girls by a socially prominent father "too busy with his briefs," as she put it, to notice what she and the rest of the family did—a father who favored her brother at her expense.

The young Dickinson was fond of that brother, of course, but she stood up to Austin, too, in ways my students were no doubt heartened by. Upset that he had not corresponded with her, she once wrote him from school not to give her the silent treatment:

> The next time you aren't going to write me, I'd thank you to let me know—this kind of *protracted* insult is what no man can bear. Fight me like a man—let me have a fair shot . . . and that ends the business!

In another letter, responding to Austin's insistence that she use a simpler and, one senses, more "feminine" style of writing, she simmered with irony:

> As simple as you please, the simplest sort of simple—I'll be a little ninny, a little pussy catty, a little Red Riding Hood; I'll wear a bee in my bonnet, and a rose-bud in my hair, and what remains to do you shall be told hereafter.

In these letters and others, Emily Dickinson made it plain that even as a schoolgirl, she had no interest in the 19th-century ideal of well-behaved and compliant femalehood. Her rejection of that ideal appears again in a letter to her friend Abiah Root which contains a tongue-in-cheek description of Abiah's classmates, together with a warning: "I expect you have a great many prim, starched up young ladies there," she wrote, "who, I doubt not, are perfect models of propriety and good behavior. If they are, don't let your free spirit be chained by them." I greatly hoped that as they read these words, my female students would think harder about what becoming models of propriety might do to their own free spirits.

Six years later, another letter to Abiah Root suggests that she had not heeded Dickinson's advice about the chains of social expectation—that in fact, Root had not understood what the advice was all about. Dickinson, now 21, the age of the seniors in my class, wrote of how different she and Root were becoming:

. . . we are growing away from each other, and
talk even now like strangers. . . . You are grow-
ing wiser than I am, and nipping in the bud
fancies which I let blossom—perchance to bear
no fruit, or if plucked, I may find it bitter. The
shore is safer, Abiah, but I love to buffet the
sea—I can count the bitter wrecks here in these
pleasant waters, and hear the murmuring winds,
but oh, I love the danger! You are learning con-
trol and firmness. Christ Jesus will love you
more. I'm afraid he don't love me *any*!

After we read the letters of this dauntless young
Dickinson to Austin and Abiah Root, it was much easier for
my class and me to find the voice and attitude of the older
Dickinson in her poems about the 19th-century's version of
womanhood–many of them poems of protest. One of my fa-
vorites still is 732, which I stumbled upon one night during
my bleary-eyed and stimulating preparations for class:

> She rose to His Requirement—dropt
> The Playthings of Her Life
> To take the honorable Work
> Of Woman, and of Wife—
>
> If ought She missed in Her new Day,
> Of Amplitude, or Awe—
> Or first Prospective—Or the Gold
> In using, wear away,
>
> It lay unmentioned—as the Sea
> Develop Pearl, and Weed,
> But only to Himself—be known
> The Fathoms they abide—

What struck me was the first line of the poem, where, by fol-
lowing the declaration "She rose" with the enjambed verb
"dropt," Dickinson slyly summarizes her poem's story of what
one woman may have lost by giving herself to "His Require-

ment"—marriage in a patriarchal society. Troubling as that possible loss is, the code of silence she has now been taken into is more troubling, compared by Dickinson to a sea, whose gender, significantly, is masculine.

Like me, my students enjoyed this poem, even though they had problems with its syntax at first—dealing, after all, with the thought process of the most original mind American poetry has yet produced. Even more difficult was the syntax of 401. In that poem Dickinson questions the values of upper-class women who are so convinced of their refinement, they are ashamed of the Deity for having created "freckled Human Nature." With a little discussion, everyone caught Dickinson's point in describing these ladies as "Soft—Cherubic Creatures" with "Dimity Convictions." But what were we to make of the grammatical complexities of the last stanza, where the poet completes her group portrait?

> It's such a common—Glory—
> A fisherman's—Degree—
> Redemption—Brittle Lady—
> Be so—ashamed of Thee—

Together, my class and I figured out that the "It" referred to "Redemption," and that given the socially superior attitude of these ladies, redemption, offered to the lowliest, would be too common a thing ever to visit them.

Struggling with these poems about women, my students began to understand that the poet we were studying was a rebel, and that part of her rebellion was aimed at the very world they had taken, more or less, for granted. The gentlewomen of 401 with their refined horror could have been the alumnae of the college who had recently cut the ribbon outside the new library, or even family relatives. The ladies of another poem we studied, 457, closed away with their gentlemen behind the doors of fashionable houses, might have been the matrons of the elegant town where the college was located—though in Dickinson's description, the houses seemed more like coffins than houses:

Sweet—safe—Houses—
Glad—gay—Houses—
Sealed so stately tight—
Lids of Steel—on Lids of Marble—
Locking Bare feet out—

Yet far from feeling threatened, my students loved Dickinson's rebellion—relished discovering the coffin-like houses and discussing whose bare feet these might have been—someone less privileged, or from the wide world of nature outdoors? Christ and the lost opportunity of redemption once again?

Turning to the Dickinson letters I liked best of all—the two she wrote to Thomas Higginson about her poetry in the spring of 1864—the class found still another possible owner of the feet: the poet herself. We began with the first and more famous of these letters, asking Higginson, a rising young man of letters, if the verse she had included was "alive." Then, since Higginson's written response no longer exists, we looked for clues to it in Dickinson's second letter to him, which clearly suggests he wanted her to rid her poems of what seemed to him eccentricities that would prevent them from being published. It was even clearer in Dickinson's second letter that she did not intend to make the changes Higginson had in mind. Faced with the alternatives of fixing up her poems for publication and preserving them as they were, however unorthodox, she wrote: "My barefoot rank is better." With poem 457 at our elbows, my class and I enjoyed the delicious picture of the barefoot genius Dickinson standing outside the "Sweet—safe" house of poetic convention.

How I loved showing my students Dickinson's defense of her poetry in her reply to Higginson! This bit of metaphor, for instance, about the effect that regularizing her verse would have on it: "While my thought is undressed, I can make the distinction; but when I put them in the gown, they look alike and numb." Or this rejection of a more conventional rhyme scheme: "I . . . could not drop the bells whose jingling cooled my tramp." Dickinson's defense of her work was all the more impressive, I told my students, because of the condition she was in when she mounted it. At the time she sent Higginson her poems, she was trying to recover from a long period of psychological darkness which she called the "terror." In asking Higginson if her verse was "alive," she was referring not only to her poetry, but to the only way she had of fully returning to life. His answer was therefore crucial to her, I said, pointing out the later sentence that linked her poetry's life to her own: "Should you think it breathed . . . I should feel quick gratitude." Psychologically fragile, and insecure about the poems she submitted to Higginson, Dickinson might have agreed to all the revisions he required, particularly given his status in the literary world. But she finally understood, I told them, that in order to save herself, she had to give every ounce of her faith to the poetry she had actually written, whether or not she became known through publication. "If fame belonged to me," I declared, quoting from Dickinson's second letter to Higginson, "I could not escape her." Looking back at the writer I was then, awakening like Dickinson—and through her—from my own despondency, and having a need for faith in my own poetry, I see how important declaiming those words was for me.

After my class and I had read about Emily Dickinson's repudiation of programs for women and social behavior, and her rejection of Higginson's systematic approach to her poetry, we were at last ready to take up her lifelong struggle with religion and the church, whose spokesmen offered still another program. In a letter written to Dr. and Mrs. J. G. Holland a few years before she left the church, she wrote:

> The minister today preached about death and judgment, and what would become of those, meaning Austin and me, who behaved improperly—and somehow the sermon scared me, and father and Vinnie looked very solemn as if the whole was true. . . . He preached such an awful sermon that I didn't much think I should see

you again until the Judgment Day, and then you would not speak to me, according to his story. The subject of perdition seemed to please him, somehow.

Another minister, whom we encountered in Dickinson's poem 1207, was a "counterfeit presence" who "preached upon 'Breadth' till it argued him narrow," since "The Broad are too broad to define." In poem 696—brought to the class's attention by a student doing a report on Dickinson's rebellion against religion—the church's system of belief was a "House of Supposition," outside of which the "timid life of Evidence/ [Kept] pleading—'I don't know.'"

Writing about the natural world outside of the church's "House," Dickinson sometimes found a belief so strong, it lifted all of our spirits—as in 214, where, amidst our ice and snow, we beheld her in a New England summer, getting so high on the "liquor" of air, sky and flower, she floated all the way to heaven. We noted, too, how ironic it was that when she arrived there, she discovered another church, where seraphs swung "their snowy Hats" and amazed saints ran to the windows to see her—"the little Tippler/ Leaning against the—Sun—" It is hard to escape the institution and decorum of religion, the poet seemed to say, even in the eternal kingdom.

Notwithstanding 214, Dickinson's search for belief in nature was not always uplifting. In 258, we found, it led to despair similar to a despair she had felt in church:

> There's a certain Slant of light,
> Winter afternoons—
> That oppresses, like the Heft
> Of Cathedral Tunes—
>
> Heavenly Hurt, it gives us—
> We can find no scar,
> But internal difference,
> Where the Meanings, are—

In other poems I assigned, and in letters too, she imagined herself lost on a stormy ocean. After the death of her mother in 1882, she wrote to Louise and Fannie Norcross, "I cannot tell how Eternity seems. It sweeps around me like a sea." And in poem 739 she played the role of a speaker whose yearning to be safe from the ocean was so strong, it created mirages of a harbor.

> I many times thought Peace had come
> When Peace was far away—
> As Wrecked Men—deem they sight the Land—
> At Centre of the Sea—
>
> And struggle slacker—but to prove
> As hopelessly as I—
> How many the fictitious Shores—
> Before the Harbor be—

Reading this poem aloud near the end of our course, I asked my class a question I had been saving all semester. Why, given all the trouble and anguish Dickinson experienced by venturing beyond the shore, wouldn't she or anyone else prefer the security and contentment of life on land? I will never forget the answer one of my students, a young woman who seldom spoke but always wore a smile, gave to the question. "Happiness," she said, "is not all there is to life." Then, without the slightest nudge from me, she went on to refer to all the smiling of the people in poem 457, whose sweet, safe houses were like coffins. As I had hoped, other students remembered that we had started our course with images of the ocean and the shore, in the letter Dickinson wrote at age 21 to the conventional Abiah Root. The risk of setting out to sea, everyone ardently agreed, was much preferable to not setting out at all.

Now, twenty years after I discovered Emily Dickinson, having become, for better or worse, the poet she helped me to be, I wonder about the students who discovered her with me. Do they still remember how we came together in that windowless basement room to study the code of her inner life, and relate it to our own? And did they all, in spite of their youthful enthusiasm for the risks of leaving the land, end up living their lives on the shore, as status-conscious parents and relatives had also done? Or did one or two—the most a teacher can expect out of any class—forsake their Abiah Root selves as Dickinson would have wished, rejecting safety for the chance to buffet the sea?

Letters from a Poet

Nearly twenty-five years ago, Donald Hall sent me a letter I reread so often I almost knew it by heart. The letter said he was glad my friends, two of my former high-school students, had brought me to his house to meet him, and he was glad I lived nearby. It also said he liked the poems of the chapbook manuscript I had left him. "Dazzled" was the word he used: "I am dazzled by your poems." This was the sentence I reread for—along with the paragraph that followed, inviting me to visit him again so we could talk about them. It was the most wonderful invitation I had ever gotten as a writer—better even than the one extended one rainy day a decade earlier by John Nims, my teacher at Bread Loaf, who slowed his black Mercedes to a stop, rolled down the window, and asked me to present my poems with four or five members of his "Craft of Poetry" class at a public reading in the Barn—better than the invitation from David Wagoner, who accepted my first poem for publication in *Poetry Northwest* shortly thereafter and wrote to request more poetry, adding *please* that when I sent my work this time, I include a self-addressed, stamped envelope.

It is fortunate that I still recall the contents of Don's first letter, because having it out so many times to reread it, I finally lost it. All the other letters he sent me during the late 1970s and early 80s I deposited one by one in a box for safe-keeping. Some concerned his work and writing life; many were about poems I had sent him for his comments. All were essential to my development, helping me to believe in myself as a poet.

Elated as I was by the generosity Don had shown me, I didn't realize that at the time, he was renewing his own belief in poetry. Having just resigned from a tenured position at the University of Michigan and moved into his ancestral home in New Hampshire with Jane Kenyon, he was a poet of technical skill who had yet to realize his full powers. Soon he would publish *Kicking the Leaves*, laying claim to his New Hampshire property through new poems about family and the past that grounded him at last as a poet and made his later and best work possible. These were the poems he was working on as we exchanged our initial letters.

I vividly remember how hopeful Don was for *Kicking the Leaves*. Sitting in a favorite chair in his living room during one of my visits, he crossed his fingers—then, in a comic follow-up, crossed his arms and legs, turning his whole body into the shape of a pretzel. Weren't established writers supposed to be more assured about what they had done? Not long after seeing Don as a pretzel, I received a large manila envelope from him and drew out of it some of the poems planned for the collection. The accompanying note asked the incredible: Would I please read them and offer whatever thoughts I had about revision? What in the world could I do to help him understand his work better, he being him, and I being me?

In particular, Don wanted to know about the long poem that concluded the book, "Stone Walls." I searched the poem for something I might tell him about it. Did I misread, or was it overly long and prosy? Not daring to say so, I confined my suggestions to the poem's ending. A few weeks afterward, in the late spring of 1977, Don wrote to tell me he was doing just what I would have told him to do in the first place if I'd had the nerve—making big cuts in the poem because it moved "too slowly" and had, as he put it, "too much repetition in it, or at least too much of the same thing. Too much fact, too much detail." Nor was "Stone Walls" the only poem from *Kicking the Leaves* Don redrafted that spring. Speaking of the rewrites both he and Jane were working on—she for her first book, *From Room to Room*—he declared: "There are revisions going on all over this house." Don's dedication to the truth of the poem above all else, no matter how many drafts the poem took, finally emboldened me to write whatever I saw fit about the poems he sent me for comment, and to go even further than I had before with revisions of my own poems.

From Don's letters, I also began to learn that being a writer meant one had to work at it. Taking a brief vacation in Bermuda with Jane in early 1978 after their books were mostly ready for publication, he was soon back at his desk spending twelve and fourteen-hour days. "We saw some palm trees and flowering shrubs and felt some warm rain," he wrote. "It was OK—but I love this eight-foot snow pile we live in." From that desk under the New Hampshire snow pile Don was producing much more than poetry—not only because he had other interests as a writer, but because without his monthly check from the University of Michigan, writing was paying the bills. In fact, the exceptional diversity of his work dates back to his beginning as a freelancer when the two of us first corresponded. His letters mention the publication of articles and book reviews, textbooks, books of essays, and his well known children's book, *The Ox-Cart Man*, which received the Caldecott prize, and which in turn funded their new bathroom named, he reported cheerfully, the "Caldecott Room."

For all the success, though, there were difficulties. "When you are freelance writing," he wrote me, "so many great ideas fall apart and bring in no mortgage-helpers" at all. Sometimes he agreed to do things as a freelancer that he later regretted. So, during the spring of 1980, after leaving the academic world behind, he consented to test his revision of a composition textbook by teaching a related course that next fall at Colby-Sawyer College, where I myself taught. On September third Don wrote me in torment: "A week from today I teach my first class. This Friday I go to a department meeting. I know it is ridiculous, disgusting, and revolting—but I *practically* feel sorry for myself, and here I am teaching only one course in three years! Do not tell anybody my disgusting secret."

Of course, these seemed like happy problems to a writer like me, struggling to publish his first book manuscript. That manuscript, grown from the chapbook I'd left on the kitchen table in Wilmot to a full collection by late 1978, was the subject of several of Don's early letters. Mainly he advised me to stop worrying about my rejection slips and get to work. "The writing—I don't need to tell you—is what matters," he wrote in June of 1979. "Keep getting better, and improve the manuscript every time it comes back, and you will win through." Two years later, in May of 1981, as I continued with the collection, he suggested more patience and more work on the book's poems: "continue to change it," he told me; "make it the best book possible."

Yet Don's most moving counsel in this period was not an upbeat call to discipline and work, but the bittersweet commiseration he offered in a letter dated July 8, 1980, which mixes advice to me in my disappointment about not yet publishing a book with the disappointment he himself had begun to feel after publishing several: "Believe me, " the letter says,

> I am sympathetic with your feelings, but let me tell you that when you have published abook— *nothing will happen*; or at least it will seem that nothing has happened. . . . Even if something happens, then you realize that the "something" is truly nothing. And after you have published eight books of poems, you are still convinced that nobody reads you, and that probably you are no good anyway. Or at least you are convinced of that frequently. I have been going through quite a bad patch, in my feelings about my own ability, my past work, and certainly my present work.
>
> There is only one place, or one moment, in which one finds happiness, and it is always momentary—because that is the moment of the actual writing, and of course that [moment] is not always true.
>
> So I do two things: I assure you that you will publish; and I tell you that it will not make any difference! But I do have a third thing to say: it makes a difference to me!

What younger poet wouldn't welcome those final, generous words? I certainly did. Yet I was also worried by Don's depression over his work, which, as it turned out, stayed with him for several months. His son's serious car accident in late 1980 did not help his mood. A record of the disturbance this accident caused him appears in a poem Jane included in her second volume of verse, *The Boat of Quiet Hours*. Called "Evening in a Country Inn," the poem shows Don smoking and pacing in the inn's long hallway. "I know you are thinking of the accident," the speaker says, "of picking the slivered glass from his hair." Don wrote me in December about his son's hospitalization, and again in January. Later letters contained bad news about Jane's father, who suffered from cancer during 1981 and died in the fall of that year.

Faced with personal sorrows and discouragement about his writing, Don did exactly what he had earlier advised me to do: He carried on with the work. How busy he could be is revealed in this excerpt from a letter written shortly before the time of his trouble:

> In the last few days, I have mailed a two-thousand word article to *The Nation*; a treatment of "film" for a textbook; and a three-thousand word article on Robert Giroux for the *New York Times Book Review*. I have finished drafting six thousand words for *Country Journal*, [and] twenty thousand words of an appendix for a textbook. . . . I have been writing twenty to thirty pages a day, and revising earlier draft on the same days.

This list would have been much longer if Don, a tireless correspondent, had referred to the letters he had written— including, of course, the one from which I just quoted. That letter was a page and a half long, and its main subject was not the work he had been doing, but poems I had sent him. In fact, my poems were the main subject of nearly all his letters to me in this period. I am pleased to report that I commented on a great many of Don's poems in the late 70s and early 80s, too, but his comments had a greater range and variety of tone than mine did. Often the advice he gave was about my poetry's language. "Can't you hear Bing Crosby singing [this] word [of yours] 'yearning'?" he asked me about one poem. "[It's] Tin Pan Alley. And the word also reminds me of the most prosperous poet ever to emerge from Tin Pan Alley . . . I mean Rod McKuen." Once, after seeing an extensive and self-adoring biographical note I had sent to *Poetry* magazine with two of my poems, Don wrote: "I think it is wise" not to load on the "fellowships or academic appointments." If I were you, he added, "I'd try something that is quite reticent, non-academic, and non 'successful,'" like: "'Wesley McNair lives in New Hampshire where he raises goats with eyes in the middle of their foreheads.'" In another letter, he recommended the poetic practice of waiting: "hold poems back for a long time before sending them even to a friend," he said, because a poem "has a way of changing *on its own*, before anybody else's words get into it. I think," he added, "you already do this."

He was right. As the poet who was still working on a collection he despaired of ever publishing, I had, in fact, developed all the expertise in waiting I would ever need. But then something wonderful happened. In the summer of 1983, I got a call from the University of Missouri Press saying my book, *The Faces of Americans in 1853*, had won the Devins Award and would be published in six months. I remember even now Don's first words when I called to tell him this sudden news. "Wes," he said, "I could kiss you." I could have kissed him also, grateful as I was in that moment. For that matter, I could have kissed the first ten people I saw.

I remember the excitement I felt going to dinner with my wife Diane and Don and Jane to celebrate my good fortune. Yet when I review my letters from Don, I find no mention of my first book—only a reference to my second book. Discovering that I had told the interviewer of a local newspaper I wanted to have a new book out by the next spring, he wrote emphatically: "try terribly hard not to rush the second book! Absolutely everybody, and not only Wes McNair who has had to wait so damn long tends to rush the second book. I myself did." But do not, "please, shoot for April."

In the matter of not rushing to publish in either books or magazines, Don was, as in other matters, a model. A year before that letter, with no new book of his own for four years, he wrote me that he was nowhere near ready for a new volume. "You know," he said, "I have not written a satisfactory poem—virtually not a poem—since *Kicking the Leaves*. . . . But," he added, "I am working on long and ambitious things, and maybe they will not only be publishable but Immortal. And after all, that is the only thing worth thinking about." I understand now that the "long and ambitious things" he was holding back were the poems he finally printed as a group no less than six years afterward in a book called *The One Day*, one of the best volumes of poems he has yet published. In the end, Don taught me this valuable lesson about the timing of book publication, which I have often pondered since: The important thing is not when you publish a book, or even how many books you publish, but the development of the poetic vision you put into the books, and the truth of that vision. Thus, the vocation of poetry is different from a game of basketball.

Given Donald Hall's voluminous correspondence, it is a safe guess that this man who once gave up a university position in poetry has gone on to instruct many other poets by letter. It is this final lesson of passing on what one knows about the craft that comes back to me now when I teach or edit or write advice of my own to an aspiring poet. I remember Don's early letter that said my poems made a difference to him, and all the other letters he wrote years ago, and I think of the great difference they made to me.

Advice for Beginning Poets

Ultimately, every poem is a love poem. Write out of humor, sorrow or anger, but write out of love.

*

If you want your poem to matter to the reader, make sure it is involved—by subject, application of subject, or both—with people other than yourself, even if your poem speaks with an "I."

*

How should your poem begin? Where possible, "in medias res," as Horace recommended.

*

Free verse makes its appeal not only to the ear, but to the eye. Break lines and arrange stanzas to show the mind at work on the page shaping the thought of your poem. The space around the poem in free verse often has its own visual meaning. Make that wordlessness articulate.

*

Mary Oliver speaks of the poem as an "enactment." Frank Bidart says that the poem imitates an action and is itself an action. In developing your poem, find the action and a climactic order for it, considering at the same time how the action may be shaped to suggest the larger meanings you have in mind. As you write, make action and your syntax unfold as one.

*

But don't start writing a poem too early. Scribble ideas, lists of images, random lines to invite your right brain—the dreaming and conceiving self—into the process of finding your subject and approach. Resist the left brain, in love with tidiness and completion, until the preliminary writing you have done will not be easy to organize.

*

The poet does not speak in generalities, but in a code of images; thus Muriel Rukeyser links poetry to painting and other "arts of sight." Your reader should, in the fullest sense of the expression, see what you mean.

*

Thought will not be possible in your poem unless you give the feet a place to stand, the hands something to touch, the eyes a world to see.

*

Poetry is written to be spoken. Avoid writing anything you would not actually say in a reasonably articulate conversation.

*

The true poetic sentence unfolds, as Robert Frost once suggested, and to unfold will normally require a climactic order. Make your sentence climactic, and break to stress its unfolding.

*

A more appropriate term than line breaking for free verse composition might be sentence-breaking, since our purpose through end-stopping and enjambment is finally to reconstruct the sentence. Enjambed more than once, a statement in free verse may come to resemble a question.

*

Strive for tension in your free verse poem between the restless and inquisitive sentence and the line that pulls back on it. In conversation, Charles Simic once described the tension this way: "The line is Buddha; the sentence is Socrates."

*

Allow your sentence as it moves line to line the freedom to surprise you and help you make up your mind—to discover what you didn't know you knew.

*

Think of your free verse poem as a musical score, in the way Denise Levertov recommended, using lines to emphasize vocal rhythm and the pitch of intonation, and line-breaks as short intervals of silence, or rests.

*

Mainly, break the lines of your free verse on nouns, verbs, or the words that describe them.

*

As the poem begins to take shape, there is always a moment when it becomes smarter than you are, and you must be just smart enough to ask it what it wants to do.

*

The main difficulty once a poem is in motion is to make it as particular and as universal as you can, both at the same time.

*

To carry the reader to a new place in thought, the turn—that moment in the lower half of a poem when the action opens to its larger meanings—is an important device. Study the sonnet, the first poem in English with a turn (Shakespeare and Keats are a good starting point), to see how the device works. Then study the more associative poems of free verse, in which turns often multiply.

*

The old advice: understate. Describing a suicide, the culmination of his poem about Richard Cory, E. A. Robinson simply tells us that Cory "went home and put a bullet through his head." Telling about another gruesome event, the killing of a character with a large rock, William Golding says only, "His skull opened."

*

The poem being a riddle, its title shouldn't give the answer to the riddle. It must stand outside the poem telling what the piece is about, but at the same time be part of the poem, contributing to its mystery, as if it were the first line. (Often the best titles for poems come from their turns or endings, where the deeper meanings are.) Beware of *other* answers to the riddle, which, in the unrevised poem, often appear at the beginning or the end.

*

Cut.

*

A poem must mean at least two things at once. Better poems have more than two meanings. The best ones have many, which change according to the reader's mood and period of life and can never be fully fathomed.

*

Because our most demanding poems ask us to think in ways that are entirely new to us, they are often hard to conclude. Allow your poem the time it needs for the right conclusion—which means, allow yourself time to complete the new thought.

*

If you have doubts about the poem you have written, the kind of doubts that make you want to ask a friend what he or she thinks, don't bother. Trust the doubts.

*

The capacity to revise determines the true writer. Suspect the finished poem. Your evil twin wants your poem to be finished.

*

A poet needs to know what the rules are to understand, when inspiration requires it, how to break them. Don't be afraid to get yourself into trouble with your subject matter or your form. . . . In new struggles, beware of strategies learned in the last battle. . . . Beware, above all, the artful dodge.

*

In one of the most remarkable passages of "Song of Myself," Walt Whitman warns us that a facility with language may interfere with the truth we have to tell. Addressing his own poetic speech, he declares, "you conceive too much of articulation."

*

Write your way down into the poem and let it well up in you, revision by revision, until it is all yours. Showing your poem to someone else before it belongs to you in this way is a little like what showing his face to the camera was for the Indian, since if you do so, part of your poem will belong to another, and will be difficult to get back.

*

Be careful not to title either your poem or your collection of poems too early, lest the title become a thesis ordering you to do things that obstruct the work's true impulse.

*

Each day life will whisper into your ear some little or large thing that must be done before turning to the poem. Yet next week, when your poem is still unwritten, you will not remember why these things were so important, or even what they were. Write your poem.

*

In this period of the public reading, your poem may have its most successful publication from the lectern; yet good readers are few. The best engage their audience expressively, yet without histrionics, speaking the poem's lines in such a way as to let the poem speak for itself.

*

Most effective poems in free verse break lines to emphasize the pauses the voice might make as the speaker "thinks" the poem's sentences; therefore, the effective public reading will be slow enough to give these pauses the appropriate vocal emphasis, and fast enough to make the audience aware that there is a sentence underway. The audience must be able to hear the tension between the sentence pressing ahead, and the line tugging back on it.

*

I have just spent a day with three participants in a nearby summer workshop, who have participated in past summer workshops. They are full of talk about who said what about which story in their shared class. They drop the names of writing teachers and ponder their reputations. And of course they carry their manuscripts—some stories, the first draft of a novel, a sheaf of poems—in the hope that someone important will read them and make them famous. What I don't have the courage to tell them—what they need to be told—is that writing is not a social activity, but a solitary one. They need to go home and practice being by themselves for long periods of time with pencil and paper.

*

The Americanization of writing over the past forty years has involved first the invention of the term "creative writing" for all imaginative work; second, the formulation of a how-to process for creative writing; and third, the socialization of the creative writing process through the workshop. Those who take part in the resulting system should be aware it offers only one way to become a writer, and that way is relatively untried.

*

Yet teachers can give memorable guidance. At the English School at Bread Loaf, John Nims, who taught creative writing in the old style, would sometimes read a student's poem aloud in class, then look up over his glasses and remark: "There's less here than meets the eye." Once he defined the poem as "a real voice in a real body in a real world."

*

Just finishing his stint as a teacher at a writers' conference, Bill Roorbach explains to me how difficult it is to convince students to do the deep-down, extensive revision that manuscripts in progress need. The 21-year-old, who is in love with his work and has not yet known revision in his own life, can't see the use of it. The 65-year-old, who has revised his life often, can see the use of it, but questions whether he has the energy and time the job requires. "I tried to tell an older woman she did have the energy and time, in spite of her misgivings," Roorbach says. "After my long pep talk, I discovered I was talking to myself about my own novel."

*

Visiting the University of New Hampshire one day in the early sixties, I was drawn to the doorway of a lecture hall by a passionate voice speaking about poetry. It turned out the voice belonged to a young man in a suit, whose subject was the damage T. S. Eliot had done to American verse; I learned only later the man was W. D. Snodgrass, invited because he had won the Pulitzer Prize in poetry. After he had derided Eliot's obscurantism and that of his models, the French symbolists, he put forth a new model, Geoffrey Chaucer, pointing out Chaucer's accessibility and his sympathy for everyday life. For me, feeling the tyranny of Eliot's influence, the lecture was inspirational. Months later, I would find it echoed in Karl Shapiro's *In Defense of Ignorance.* Years later, I would find a way to put the ideas I heard to use. But listening to a beardless Snodgrass in that doorway, I saw for the first time the possibility of my own poetry.

*

Right in the middle of my excitement after publishing my first book of poems, an aging Richard Eberhart made me consider the difficulty of acquiring readers for what I had written. Had I ever thought of how hard it was to make my mark in a period when there were so many poets? he wanted to know. "When I began, it was easy," he said. "There were only a few of us."

*

Nothing is harder for writers young or old than to keep faith with their work despite rejection. For assistance, memorize this by Robert Francis on the subject of editorial judgment: "In the eyes of eternity, it may be the editor and not the little poem that was weighed in the balance and found wanting."

*

It is difficult to know and accept the materials your life experience has given you for your poetry—easier to avoid them as threatening, or question them as inadequate. Yet you will have no others. Embrace them; they are the source of your truth and power as a poet.

*

No one teaches us more about the value of the heart in the creation of our spiritual and creative life than John Keats in his letters. In order to develop the soul, he once wrote, it is necessary for the heart to "feel and suffer in a thousand diverse ways."

*

The poet's difficult contract: To have heartbreaking powers, the world must first break your heart. No poet ever said, "You may enter my heart, but first wipe your feet and agree to behave."

*

Your highest calling is not to publish your poems or become famous for them, but to shape your experience into a vision of life. This will take as long as you have on earth. Be patient. Don't lacerate yourself. And keep in mind battle cries of poets who have come before you. Walt Whitman: "stand up for the stupid and the crazy." Adrienne Rich: "break open the locked chambers of possibility, restore numbed zones to feeling, recharge desire." Muriel Rukeyser: "we are ready for the poems of our true life."

*

How can we understand the world that has been given to us? From the beginning, spiritual advisers have told us the only way is to settle down and be still. The stillness that the act of writing itself requires is only the beginning of this process. Be still not only in the room where you write, but in the place where you live, coming to know it by your unknowing relationship with it. In this way, you will come to know the world.

MAPPING THE HEART

III.
Map Makers

Taking the World for Granite
FOUR POETS IN NEW HAMPSHIRE

When I look back on the work of poets I came to know in New Hampshire in the 70s and 80s, I am surprised to discover that in the very period I was attempting to make poems about the people and places of the region around me in the granite state, they were all doing the same thing. The poets I have in mind are four of our important ones—Maxine Kumin, Jane Kenyon, Donald Hall, and Charles Simic. As far as I know, nothing much has been made of the fact that the vision of these poets has been influenced by a patch of ground no more than seventy-five miles square, but I find the fact remarkable, and worth at least a few words.

Not one of these New Hampshire interpreters is a native; all spent much of their lives outside the state. Born in Philadelphia, Maxine Kumin was a resident of suburban Boston before she arrived, buying an abandoned farm in Warner in the 60s, and living there summers until she made it her permanent home in 1976. The amusing and ironic sign visitors find on her barn, "POBIZ FARM," tells a lot about the life in poetry she has found since. It suggests not only that Kumin's poetry business has helped to sustain the farm, but that the natural life of the farm is the main business of her poetry. In fact, Maxine Kumin's experience over the past thirty years on her 200-acre property has transformed her into one of this country's principal poets of nature.

Like Hall and Kenyon, Maxine Kumin laid claim to her property as a poet in a particular book—in her case, *Up Country: Poems of New England,* published in 1974. The book begins with the well known "hermit" poems, in which Kumin plays

the role of a recluse in retreat from society—a role parallel-
ing her own departure from the Boston suburbs, not to men-
tion the flight from Concord, Massachusetts, undertaken a
century earlier by her longstanding model Henry David
Thoreau. In the guise of the hermit, Kumin explores and
discovers the nature of the territory she has chosen for her
new residence. Thereby, she introduces themes about the
relationship between humans and the natural world that is
central in all of her later volumes of poetry.

One of these themes is the need to coexist with nature's
creatures. In "The Hermit Picks Berries," Kumin's character
illustrates the concept as he attends to the behavior of ani-
mals and learns from them:

> At midday the birds doze.
> So does he.
>
> The frogs cover themselves.
> So does he . . .
>
> The snake uncoils its clay self
> in the sun on a rock in the pasture.
> It is the hermit's pasture.
> He encourages the snake.

The importance of the female principle in Kumin's na-
ture also begins with the hermit poems. So various creatures
in the hermit sequence are female and linked with procre-
ation or nurture. Kumin's resonant image of the nest in "The
Hermit Prays" underscores the ideal of nature's femaleness:

> I hold in my hand this cup
> this ritual, this slice of womb
> woven of birchbark strips
> and the woolly part of a burst cocoon
> all mortared with mud and chinked
> with papers of snakeskin.

What happens when nature's femaleness is violated, a recurring theme in Kumin's poetry after *Up Country*, is shown by two of that book's poems. In one of them, "The Vealers," the female is under attack. The poem explains how calves raised for milk are taken from their mothers after birth and placed in individual pens where milk "comes on schedule in a nippled pail." The result is torment for calves and cows alike:

> . . . Bleating racks the jail.
>
> Across the barn the freshened cows
> answer until they forget who is there.
> Morning and night, machinery
> empties their udders. Grazing allows
> them to refill. The hungry
> calves bawl and doze sucking air.

In "Woodchucks," the narrator becomes so obsessed with woodchucks damaging her garden that she gasses their underground homes and turns on them with her .22, killing two babies and their mother:

> I . . . drew a bead on the littlest woodchuck's face.
> He died down in the everbearing roses.
>
> Ten minutes later I dropped the mother. She
> flipflopped in the air and fell, her needle teeth
> still hooked in a leaf of early Swiss chard.
> Another baby next . . .

Violating the female force in nature and the hermit's principle of coexistence, Kumin's violent narrator fails twice.

Despite human lapses, however, *Up Country* strongly affirms our relationship with animals, just as all of Kumin's books ultimately do. Nowhere in this defining volume is the affirmation clearer than in "Watering Trough," which praises the Yankee practice of placing old bathtubs outdoors as watering troughs for livestock. And nowhere, given the poem's subject, is Kumin's New Hampshire inspiration more evident. Here are the bathtubs in the poem's opening:

> Let the end of all bathtubs
> be this putting out to pasture
> of four Victorian bowlegs
> anchored in grasses.

It does not matter, she implies here and in later lines, that the tubs will never again be used indoors for the civilized ritual of bathing; for now, they have entered a truer existence as vessels for animals, who come to them carrying burdock and thistle, to "slaver the scum of/ timothy and clover/ on the castiron lip that/ our grandsires climbed over." Humorous as "Watering Trough" is, the poem also has a serious side, advocating the harmony between humans and creatures. For by making her bowlegged tub a comic symbol of the civilized order, and by both inviting the animals of the field to drink from the tub and us to join in her celebration of its new function, Kumin allows us to think beyond the barriers civilization has placed between us and animals, and to appreciate our connection with the creatural life.

Comparing *Up Country*'s poems about humans and creatures with their counterparts in Maxine Kumin's later books, one sees differences. The animals of the later volumes are not only from New Hampshire, but from all over the world. There are the menaced and endangered species in *Nurture*, for instance—caribou, aquatic mammals and Trumpeter swans—and in her most recent collection, *Looking for Luck*, Alaskan seals and an elephant from Thailand. Such creatures show Kumin has become more global in her concern about animals and our connections with them. In the end, though, the links to *Up Country* are unmistakable. Her nature continues to be primarily female; so her most moving poems about animals tend to be about females of the species. Kumin uses females in the later poems to illustrate nature under attack, like the manatee cows and calves of *Nurture* who die after ingesting plastic from beer-cans and metal pop-tops. And whether she writes of elephants or New Hampshire bears, Kumin carries on her advocacy of coexistence with nature's creatures. In fact, over the years since *Up Country*, through poems like "Amanda Dreams She Has Died and Gone to the Elysian Fields" and "Praise Be," she has raised that coexistence to a new level, revealing the emotional and spiritual connections that are possible in the human relationship with horses.

In 1975, twelve years after Maxine Kumin spent her first summer in Warner, Donald Hall settled less than thirty miles away at his grandfather's old farmhouse in Wilmot, where he had spent boyhood summers. Leaving behind a professorship at the University of Michigan to become a freelance writer, Hall was in the middle of his career as a poet, the author of six books whose poetry showed his versatility, but lacked a certain maturity and depth. Then came his seventh book, *Kicking the Leaves*, in which Hall, like Maxine Kumin in *Up Country*, made an imaginative claim on his New Hampshire property—a process, in his case, of connecting with family and the past. Finding his place as a poet in that volume, he went on to create his best and most original work.

Hall's claim is made in a series of poems that begins with "Maple Syrup." In this verse he explores his ancestral home, once owned by his dead grandfather, with his new wife, Jane Kenyon. They begin their exploration in the graveyard, looking for the grandfather's grave. Unable to find it, the two go inside the house, eventually ending up in its foundation, where they discover a quart of maple syrup made by the grandfather years before:

> . . . we wash off twenty-five years
> of dirt, and we pull
> and pry the lid up, cutting the stiff,
> dried rubber gasket, and dip our fingers
> in, you and I both, and taste
> the sweetness, you for the first time,

the sweetness preserved, of a dead man
in the kitchen he left
when his body slid
like anyone's into the ground.

In search of the grandfather's grave, the couple discovers his living presence, preserved in the sweetness they taste together. Significantly, the container of maple syrup is located in a "root cellar" with "enormous/ granite foundation stones," its placement indicating how deep the connection with the grandfather is in this moment, and how formative.

The connection with his grandfather initiates memories that link Hall more strongly to the life and culture of his region. In "The Black-Faced Sheep," he remembers the rituals of keeping sheep on his grandfather's farm, and ponders the influence of sheep on the generations of his family.

When the shirt wore out, and darns in the woolen
shirt needed darning,
a woman in a white collar
cut the shirt into strips and braided it,
as she braided her hair every morning.

In a hundred years
the knees of her great-granddaughter
crawled on a rug made from the wool of sheep
whose bones were mud,
like the bones of the woman, who stares
from an oval in the parlor.

* * *

I forked the brambly hay down to you
in nineteen-fifty. I delved my hands deep
in the winter grass of your hair.

In another poem about farm animals, "Names of Horses," he recalls the work of horses, recovering the folkways of ancestors in the process.

All winter your brute shoulders strained
    against collars, padding
and steerhide over ash hames, to haul
sledges of cordwood for drying through spring
    and summer,
for the Glenwood stove next winter, and for
    the simmering range . . .

Sundays you trotted the two miles to church
    with the light load
of a leather quarter top buggy, and grazed in
    the sound of hymns.

The sense of continuity such recollections give him is
reflected in the old walls he describes in "Stone Walls." Locked
together as they ascend two nearby mountains, they manifest
a durability that steadies him against the worst excesses of
the present:

    . . . the Shah of Iran's opponents
wake to discover nails
driven through their kneecaps. When Pinochet
    frowns
in Chile, hearing these howls,
the corners of his mouth twitch with an
    uncontrollable grin . . .

    Each morning we watch stone walls
emerge on Kearsarge and on Ragged Mountain;
I love these mountains which do not change.
The screams persist. I continue my life.

The conclusion of "Stone Walls" summarizes the integration
Hall comes to feel with the generations, traditions, nature,
and religious beliefs of his new place.

At Church we eat squares of bread, we
    commune with mothers
and cousins, with mothering-fathering hills,

with dead and living,
and go home in gray November, in Advent waiting,
among generations unborn
who will look at the same hills, as the leaves fall
and turn gray,
and watch stone walls ascending Ragged Mountain.

Because of the identity his place provides, Hall is able to accept, even luxuriate in, the cycles of life and death he portrays in his title poem "Kicking the Leaves," and able also, as he puts it in "Stone Walls," to "daydream only of waking the next morning" and walking "on the earth of the present/ past noons of birch and sugarbush, past cellarholes,/ many miles to the village of nightfall."

Donald Hall's remembered grandfather, a guiding spirit, moves through many of the New Hampshire poems that follow "Maple Syrup," doing farm chores, telling stories about the past, and reciting poetry, just as Hall himself would one day do. Did the regional and narrative poetry the grandfather recited offer a model of sorts for Hall as he worked on the narrative poems of *The Happy Man*, the volume that followed *Kicking the Leaves*? Whether it did or not, the impact of Hall's seventh book on all the later work is clear. The effort to understand himself in relation to family and generations leads directly to "Shrubs Burned Away," the long poem that appears in *The Happy Man* and *The One Day*, and the theme of a shared community life in *The Happy Man's* "Twelve Seasons" sequence also relies on themes in *Kicking the Leaves*. Moreover, the wholesome values and work life Hall associates with the grandfather in *Kicking the Leaves* shape his attitudes toward the despoliation of farm land and the emptiness of work in *The One Day*. Hall's recent collection, *The Museum of Clear Ideas* also bears the influence of the earlier book, particularly in its long perspective on time and history, a perspective first ventured in "Stone Walls." Like Maxine Kumin's *Up Country*, then, *Kicking the Leaves* was crucial to Hall's poetic development—not only in its themes but in its form. In fact, the extended lines and catalogs of *Kicking the Leaves,* indicating the confidence of a writer who is tapping his full depth, have been hallmarks of Donald Hall's style ever since that book was published.

It is remarkable that the great influence of *Kicking the Leaves* derives from only nine poems, long as some of those poems are. Though there are four other pieces in the book, they have little to do, as Peter Stitt once noted, with its heart and substance. Nor are all the poems of Jane Kenyon's *From Room to Room* germane to its true purpose. But the ones that are—filling most of her first volume—do what both Hall and Kumin do in their defining books: appropriate New Hampshire.

There is a good reason why the materials of the Hall and Kenyon collections are related. As husband and wife the two were writing their books in the same period at the same place—Donald Hall's ancestral farm. So Kenyon's title poem, "From Room to Room," parallels Hall's "Maple Syrup," describing, as it does, her response to the house they have chosen to settle in. But while the narrator of "Maple Syrup" finds a connection with his grandfather and a sense of location, the speaker in the Kenyon poem experiences disconnection and dislocation. For she is turned away by the very things that take him in. Left "among photographs/ of your ancestors, their hymnbooks and old/ shoes," she moves "from room to room,/ a little dazed," like a fly she sees bumping against the windows. "I am clumsy here," she says, "thrusting/ slabs of maple into the stove" and mistaking the wind against the house's clapboard for the arrival of a car in the driveway. In the poem's conclusion, she recalls a line from one of the church hymns she sings with her husband on Sundays: "Blessed be the tie that binds." Though she tries to remember how the hymn goes from there, she can only repeat the word "tie," suggesting her own predicament of being bound to this place whose meaning, special to her mate, she cannot understand. The poem concludes as the tie is transformed into an oxygen hose that tethers an astronaut, turning "out-

side the hatch,/ taking a look around." Bound and adrift as
he explores an alien world, the astronaut gives her a way to
think about herself.

In poems immediately following "From Room to Room,"
the displaced speaker tries to find her place, wondering at
the same time whether she will ever belong. In one, "This
Morning," she even has a vision of Wesley Wells in the barn:

> White breath of cows
> rises in the tie-up, a man
> wearing a frayed winter jacket
> reaches for his milking stool
> in the dark.

Yet it is not this man, so important for Hall, who finally ac-
commodates Kenyon to the New Hampshire farm; it is the
women who once lived there. Discovering things these women
have left behind, she finally forms connections with her new
region that are, in the end, not unlike the connections of *Kick-
ing the Leaves*. In "The Thimble," she chances upon a silver
thimble in the woodshed, bent oval perhaps because the woman
who wore it "shaped it to fit her finger." The object reveals to
her a link between her present experience and the past:

> Its decorative border of leaves, graceful
> and regular, like the edge of acanthus
> on the tin ceiling at church . . .
> repeating itself over our heads
> while we speak in unison
> words the wearer must have spoken.

The hair she discovers doing housework in "Finding a
Long Gray Hair" makes her aware of the work-life of earlier
women. I quote the poem in full.

> I scrub the long floorboards
> in the kitchen, repeating
> the motions of other women

who have lived in this house.
And when I find a long gray hair
floating in the pail,
I feel my life added to theirs.

These poems lead to "Hanging Pictures in Nanny's Room,"
in which Kenyon imagines the mentality and daily rituals of
an ancestor in a parlor photograph, and finally to a sequence
in part two of _From Room to Room_ recalling her own grand-
mother and mother.

The result is a journey toward belonging that continues
into the next-to-last section, "Afternoon in the House." True,
the journey there is sometimes threatened by encounters with
a dark nature—the violent storm which destroys a favorite
tree in "The Circle in the Grass," for instance, and the night-
shadows in "Full Moon in Winter" that seem to mirror the
self's struggle with the body. Yet the section and the book
itself culminate in Kenyon's longest poem, "American Trip-
tych," a celebration of life in rural New Hampshire. The
poem's three parts feature the country store where "Cousins
arrive like themes and variations"; kids playing baseball in a
hayfield, beyond "deaths or separations"; and a potluck din-
ner at the Baptist Church, whose wholesomeness restores a
sense of personal and national innocence:

> On the way home we pass the white clapboard
> faces of the library and town hall, luminous in
> the moonlight, and I remember the first time I
> ever voted—in a township hall in Michigan.
>
> That same wonderful smell of coffee was in the
> air, and I found myself among people trying to
> live ordered lives. . . . And again I am struck
> with love for the Republic.

Such visions, not unlike those of Donald Hall's long poem
"Stone Walls," open the way for the section's final poem, "Now
That We Live," whose praise of the natural world around her

farmhouse, including the "blue/ imperturbable" Mount Kearsarge, makes clear she is at last home.

The title poem of "Afternoon in the House" hints at one other journey Jane Kenyon undertakes in her first volume. A beginning poet, she is also moving "from room to room" of poetic form and metaphor, trying to locate herself as a poet even as she finds her place in rural New Hampshire. Testing everything from prose poetry to the more compressed and inward verse we have come to associate with her, she makes her way toward the integrated poetic style of her later volumes. This journey concludes with translations of Anna Akhmatova, whose imagistic technique strongly influenced Kenyon's methodology in this book and throughout her career.

So like the Kumin and Hall books, *From Room to Room* plays a vital role in Jane Kenyon's development. It reveals the start of her characteristic poem, sampled in "The Thimble" and "Finding a Long Gray Hair": the brief lyric, in which a slow accumulation of images and events leads to a concluding epiphany. The darker poems of her three later volumes also begin in this book, where narrators like those of "The Circle in the Grass" and "Full Moon in Winter" link troubling views of nature with inner distress. As for the origin of Kenyon's religious poetry, consider "Here," whose quotation from *The Book of Common Prayer* helps the speaker to accept her new place in New Hampshire, the state she drew upon for most of the poetry in *From Room to Room* and all the books that followed it.

A year before Jane Kenyon arrived in Wilmot, in 1973, I drove with a friend to the University of New Hampshire in Durham for a presentation by Charles Simic, who had been flown in from California to interview for a position in the UNH English department. Though Simic's first collection, *Dismantling the Silence*, had been out a short time, we were already familiar with its poems, which transformed simple objects like brooms and stones into mysterious mythic symbols. We went to Durham to hear him read that work, and more like it from his new book, *Return to a Place Lit by a Glass of Milk.* Later, after Simic was hired at the state university and settled in Strafford, a change—more gradual than those of the other poets in this essay—occurred in his work. In books like *Weather Forecast for Utopia and Vicinity, Poems 1967-82* and *Austerities,* he began to fold into his characteristic mixture of folklore and archetype allusions to twentieth-century life and history. Sometimes those references related to his experience as a boy in Eastern Europe, during and after the Second World War. But they also related directly to his experience in his adopted state of New Hampshire. Through them, he revealed what he has called the "uncertainty" of today's world, where hope is difficult for many to come by, and neither justice nor moral guidance seems to exist.

The New Hampshire locations Simic chose as he shaped this later poetry were not well-scrubbed towns like the one in Jane Kenyon's "American Triptych" or farmhouses like Donald Hall's, blessed by family tradition; they were more ragged places whose citizens lived out their lives in poverty and unfulfillment. Various scenes from "A Fall Day" provide examples. In that poem, "lean dogs" from a trailer park chase a "slumped/ Figure hands deep in his pockets receding on the/ Gravelly road"; an aging woman combs her "Graying hair under the dead/ Clock"; and "Naked truth [looks] out/ Vacant-eyed on the rain-/ Blurred weedchoked outskirts/ Of a dying milltown." Another New Hampshire scene appears in "Winter Night," where a church, unlike the comforting churches of Hall and Kenyon, is compared to "an iceberg." The frightening figure knocking at its door turns out to be a drunk man who seeks relief, but is denied entrance:

> The monster created by mad Dr. Frankenstein
> Sailed for the New World,
> And ended up some place like New Hampshire.
>
> Actually, it's just a local drunk,
> Knocking with a snow-shovel,
> Wanting to go in and sit.

An iceberg is a large, drifting
Piece of ice, broken off a glacier.

"The Great Horned Owl," features another luckless man
who seeks relief. I quote the poem whole:

> One morning the Grand Seigneur
> Is so good as to appear.
> He sits in a scrawny little tree
> In my backyard.
>
> When I say his name aloud,
> He turns his head
> And looks at me
> In utter disbelief.
>
> I show him my belt,
> How I had to
> Tighten it lately
> To the final hole.
>
> He ruffles his feathers,
> Studies the empty woodshed,
> The old red Chevy on blocks.
> Alas! He's got to be going.

The junk car, the empty woodshed, the man going without—
all are well known in Simic's region. Adding his "Grand
Seigneur" to these local materials, he creates a symbolic story
which questions whether the powers that be in the universe
care about human misfortune—or whether, given that only
the desperate speaker sees and names this strange bird, such
powers exist at all.

   The focus Simic gives to the empty woodshed in the
poem suggests that winter is coming—one more threat for
his narrator. In fact, late fall and winter, seasons that take up
most of the year in New Hampshire, are common in the po-
ems of *Weather Forecast for Utopia and Vicinity* and *Austerities.*
"Northern Exposure" speaks of the "grayness of . . . remain-

ing daylight" before a snowfall; "A Fall Day," of "Late autumn already grainy/ Gritty"; and "February," in which an unnamed figure lights a woodstove, of cold and "glacial stillness." Such seasonal backdrops together with the grayness or darkness that often accompany them are well suited to the bleak vision the poems express.

One further example of a winter backdrop appears in "Crows." There, Simic observes the "Absolutely necessary/ Way" crows shake snow from their wings, holding them out as if to make a sign. The gesture of the crows in this poem is a little like the gesture in Robert Frost's famous poem, "Dust of Snow":

> The way a crow
> Shook down on me
> A dust of snow
> From a hemlock tree
>
> Has given my heart
> A change of mood
> And saved some part
> Of a day I had rued.

Simic's poem also recalls Maxine Kumin, who so often writes about nature's creatures. But where both Frost in his poem and Kumin in many of hers find a connection with the natural world, Simic ultimately finds only "enigma," unable to tell whether or not there is meaning in the "two large algebraic x's" the crows make "As if for emphasis" or just "the mockery of" meaning.

What impact did New Hampshire poems like "Crows" have on Charles Simic's later work? Clearly, they helped to open it, in Hawthorne's phrase, to an "intercourse with the world." Exactly how much the state continues to influence his poetry is difficult to tell. Today's Simic poem is ladled from a stew of such various ingredients—now including intellectual and religious history—one cannot always say for sure what combinations it contains. Still, specific references to New

Hampshire have continued, in poems such as "Department of Public Monuments" from *Unending Blues,* featuring a fat woman "In faded overalls/ Outside a house trailer/ On a muddy road to some place called Pittsfield or Babylon"; or "Winter Sunset" from *The Book of Gods and Devils,* with its ominous scene of the First Congregational church in a deserted village, clutching a weathervane against winter's dying day.

In such scenes, I recognize him as the poet who lives in New Hampshire, sharing the state with the three other poets of this essay. How close these poets are to each other in their towns of Strafford, Wilmot and Warner; yet in the inspiration they have taken from their small patch of ground, they are often far apart. In fact, the most remarkable part of their story is not finally that place has influenced them, but that they have imagined such diverse roles to express their sense of place: Kumin as a hermit, Hall as a boy feeding sheep, Kenyon as the astronaut in a farmhouse, and Simic cinching his belt for a great horned owl.

A Government of Two

Two or three years ago, something happened to my friends Donald Hall and Jane Kenyon that I'd never seen in the literary world before. Up to that time each was well known to poetry audiences—he as a senior American poet and recent recipient of the National Book Critics Circle Award, she as a younger poet with a growing reputation. Then, their relationship itself became famous. Through their co-readings, their joint interviews in print and on the NPR show *Fresh Air*, and most importantly, their starring roles in the Bill Moyers special, *A Life Together*, millions of Americans came to know of the life in poetry the two shared as husband and wife in rural New Hampshire. Audiences also became aware of the couple's sorrows: Kenyon's life-long struggle with depression, and Hall's colon cancer, which metastasized to the liver and despite a successful operation, seemed likely to return. Later on, of course, those who had followed the Hall-Kenyon story learned of its ironic and heart-rending conclusion: fearing the fatal recurrence of his disease, the couple discovered a cancer growing in her—the leukemia that, despite a bone-marrow transplant, finally killed her, and left him with a grief that has lasted to this day.

The moving and ultimately tragic story of their life together has created a new interest in the poetry of Hall. It has created even more interest in Kenyon, whose death in mid-career has not only cast a spell upon many readers, but caused confusion about her work. I have heard readers attribute a variety of melancholy poems to her bout with leukemia, when in fact only one poem, "The Sick Wife," was written in the months of her fatal illness. Compounding the error, the review of her new and selected volume *Otherwise* in *Publishers Weekly* asserted that all of the book's new poems were about "her pending death." Yet if the legendary story of Kenyon and Hall makes her verse and his harder to see and assess, that story also suggests a new way to examine their poetry. For the truth is, their life together was vital to their development as poets, influencing everything from work methods to the content of work produced. In fact, it made their best poems possible.

To say so is only to repeat what these poets have suggested themselves. In a joint interview by Marian Blue printed in the *AWP Chronicle* shortly before Kenyon's death, Hall remarked, "The great changes in my poetry, which my friends and the book reviewers find beginning in *Kicking the Leaves*, began after our marriage, while we were still in Ann Arbor; the move [to his family farmhouse] confirmed, enlarged, and extended those changes." And Kenyon declared: "whatever it is that I know about writing poems, I have learned most of it from being with Don, moving to his ancestral farm, keeping my ears open when his peers come to visit."

As I have mentioned in earlier sections of this book, I became aware of their relationship when I myself visited that New Hampshire farm shortly after they moved in, drawn by hopes for my own poetry. Living nearby in New Hampshire, I knew that Hall had arrived at the place the year before, but I did not know much about Jane Kenyon, and neither did the friends who brought me there; it was the established poet and anthologist Donald Hall we had gone to see. However, Hall soon made it clear he was not the only writer living in the farmhouse. Inviting me back a couple of days later to discuss some poems I had left with him, he not only told me that Kenyon wrote poetry, but that she had her own assessment of my poems, which he, in her absence, passed on with obvious respect.

I should have sensed then how valuable she had become to him as a reader of his own work, but I thought mostly about how valuable he was to hers. The Jane Kenyon I became ac-

quainted with at that time was, after all, very much like me—
a young writer in formation who needed the kind of support
an older writer like Hall, generous to a fault, offered—namely,
the assurance that one had talent; the encouragement to use
the talent; and honest, experienced appraisals of work in
progress. Hall was helping both of us in these ways in the
same period, and because he was supporting Kenyon
financially, she had the additional luxury of free time.

Of course, Kenyon received help early and late in her
career from other writers, as Hall himself did. In 1983 she
began to attend regular workshop sessions with Peseroff and
the poet and fiction writer Alice Mattison. Whereas the groups
Hall worked with, assembled by correspondence, shifted
membership over the years, Kenyon's, which she jokingly
called "The Committee," never changed. According to
Mattison, meeting with her group in the early period demon-
strated to Kenyon that Hall's was not the only approach to
poetry and made it easier for her to disagree with his assess-
ments of her poems, despite his seniority. "No poem is finished
until it has been passed by the Committee," Kenyon often
declared. Yet as useful as Peseroff and Mattison were to
Kenyon throughout her career (and the influence they had
on both her attitude as a poet and the development of par-
ticular poems was considerable), the range of Hall's assistance
ultimately made him more useful to her than even the Com-
mittee was. Besides, Hall gave her early and late the model of
extraordinary devotion to his art.

"I think," he wrote to me recently, "I helped her in one
big way, always: the hard work, the dedication, the stubborn-
ness, the ambition." It is clear to me from my experience that
he is right. When I met her, several years before the Commit-
tee first convened, she kept no regular writing schedule, but
she was already beginning to write more than she had be-
fore. There is no doubt her new application came from watch-
ing Hall spend ten or more hours every day on poetry and
prose, rain or shine, in hope and disappointment. Through
him, she came to know how the writing life worked, and how

the poems got done. "Don has so many poems, he could easily give several readings and never read the same poem twice," she told me as she was counting up poems for her first book, nearly complete. "All I have is these," she said. I see now that even as she measured her small output against Hall's, she was pondering the challenge of gathering more poems in her future. And when her first volume was at last ready and she had trouble placing it with a publisher, I heard Hall assure her that "It will happen" in a tone that suggested her own career in poetry would happen, too.

As Kenyon herself remarked, Hall's influence included the "peers" he introduced her to at his farm. One of these was Robert Bly, who advised her in the late 1970s to work on translations of the Russian poet Anna Akhmatova—probably the most important single piece of advice she ever received as a poet. Through Bly and another of Hall's friends, Louis Simpson, Kenyon located a translator, Vera Dunham, to help her with the project, publishing six Akhmatova poems in her first volume of poetry (1978), and more of them in *Twenty Poems of Anna Ahkmatova* (1980). As a result of her translations, Kenyon discovered the possibilities of the brief lyric, which she was to explore for the rest of her writing life.

In the introduction to *Twenty Poems* she describes not only Akhmatova's early poetry, but the verse she herself was now attempting. Interestingly, her description refers to John Keats, her other major influence at this time:

> As we remember John Keats for the beauty and intensity of his shorter poems,especially the odes and the sonnets, so we may revere Ahkmatova for her early lyrics—brief, perfectly-made verses of passion and feeling. Images build emotional pressure. . . . I love the sudden twists these poems take, often in the last line.

The poem Kenyon cites for illustration is one I heard her recite at a reading the two of us did together, with Hall in attendance, perhaps four years after *Twenty Poems* appeared:

We walk along the hard crest of the snowdrift
toward my white, mysterious house,
both of us so quiet,
keeping the silence as we go along.
And sweeter even than the singing of songs
is this dream, now becoming real:
the swaying of branches brushed aside
and the faint ringing of your spurs.

I recall how, in the question-and-answer session that followed our reading, she went back to the poem, taking pleasure in the "sudden twist" of its conclusion, where simple images are charged with eroticism. And I remember that she asked Hall at the restaurant we went to afterward about the poems she read from her first book *From Room to Room*, now several years old. He thought they had held up well, but Kenyon had her doubts. Of course, she had by that time experienced harrowing personal difficulties, including the death of her father and serious episodes of mania and depression—difficulties that changed her as a poet and must have altered her view of the earlier work. But I see now her doubts came also from her encounter with Ahkmatova, who had changed the way she worked so much as to make some of her first poems seem foreign to her. I would discover the results of that encounter later on with the publication of her second book, *The Boat of Quiet Hours*, akin to Ahkmatova's early work not only in its method but its content: the allusive imagery drawn from nature or domestic life, the dreamy speech, the tone of anguish or melancholy.

Another thing I did not grasp at the time of our joint reading was the full meaning of Donald Hall's expression the whole time Jane read—a combination of the greatest pride and joy. It was the same expression I noticed at later readings when he sat in the audience; I took it then, as before, to be a sign of the pleasure her progress as a poet gave him, as it surely was. But reading this comment by Hall in the *AWP Chronicle*'s interview makes me now suspect that the pleasure Hall took at her readings and in the letters he sent to me over the years praising her work, was more complicated than I initially thought, and related to his own progress as a poet:

> I know I have been encouraged and thrilled to watch Jane's own poetry develop, mature, become better and better. . . . Possibly in rivalry, possibly in mere joy, I think I have responded to her own increasing ambition and excellence by trying even harder myself, or perhaps with more energy.

In fact, as I return to the poetry Hall started with *Kicking the Leaves*, no longer focusing on the older poet who guided both Kenyon and me but on a writer with his own need to change and grow, I see the help his wife gave him as an artist was every bit as valuable as the assistance he gave her. Even as he was providing a model for her as an older writer with long-term experience, she was presenting him with the model of a young writer developing and thriving. And just as he helped her by the discipline he brought to his craft, she helped him, as he put it to me in a letter, "by her own stubbornness and by the example of her overcoming obstacles, personal and emotional ones, to make art"—also "by her stubborn and beautiful love of the art of poetry."

It is now clear to me, moreover, that whereas Hall's influence on the content of Kenyon's poetry was limited, Kenyon's influence on the content of his was profound. Only through his relationship with her in his ancestral farmhouse was he able to imagine the connection with Kate and Wesley Wells and their agrarian past that is essential to *Kicking the Leaves*. It is Kenyon, after all, with whom he dunks his finger into the quart of syrup in the central poem "Maple Syrup," the two of them bonding through that gesture with the grandfather and the past; and it is Kenyon he refers to in "Flies" when he says, "We live in the house left behind; we sleep in the bed where they whispered at night." That "we," linked in the book's last poem "Stone Walls" to a vision of family and community, nature, and religious belief, is what brings the sense of place Hall celebrates into being.

In their *AWP Chronicle* interview, Hall speaks of Kenyon's influence on the "Sister" poems of his next book, *The Happy Man*, as well: "my closeness to Jane," he says, "gave me the courage to try writing in a female voice." It seems likely that Kenyon's impact on *The Happy Man* was even more extensive and began with certain poems in her first volume *From Room to Room*. In this book Kenyon identifies—through verses like "The Thimble," "Finding a Long Gray Hair," and "Hanging Pictures in Granny's Room—with the women who have lived on Hall's ancestral farm. Reading such poems one by one as Kenyon wrote them, Hall was no doubt better able to imagine an alternative, feminine view of his new place and of the world—the view that he presents in *The Happy Man*. Thus, there is an irony in the title of this volume which critics have not yet noticed: that his collection is not finally so much about a man or the masculine self as it is about woman and the power of femininity.

Hall's female principle in the book is associated with the idea of repose, a word which recurs in the poems of the last section, "Sisters," and which is defined in the section's epigraph (from Meister Eckhart) as "what the soul [looks] for" and "what all creatures [want], in all their natural efforts and motions." The male principle, on the other hand, as announced in the section titled "Men Driving Cars," has to do with compulsive motion and the submergence of the emotional and intuitive life. It is significant that men in this section, clearly the weaker sex, are disconnected from women; for the ideal the book advances in spite of its darknesses is a linking of the masculine and feminine selves, appearing in poems about grandfather and grandmother, mother and father, uncle and niece, and couples engaged and married. It should be no surprise that among the volume's couples, those most often referred to are the author himself and Jane Kenyon, the wife and poet who initiated the collection's feminine themes. Making a first appearance in *Kicking the Leaves*, this "we" has played a crucial role in every Hall book since.

In Donald Hall's next volume, *The One Day*, a book-length poem about America's spiritual corruption, he casts his couple as exemplars bound so closely in their love and their work of writing that "the day is double" and their eyes "gaze not at each other but a third thing" they have created together: "work's paradise." The poem's recurrent scenes of himself and Kenyon in their farmhouse are the more moving for being placed in the context of the lovelessness and unfulfilling work of American society. Linking his life with Kenyon to the life of the nation in *The One Day,* Hall was never before so affirmative about their relationship or more encompassing in his poetic vision. And Kenyon, who had provided him with the real-life version of the poem's relationship, helped him bring the ambitious poem forth. As his first reader, she was the one who listened to him read the poem aloud in an early draft; it was she too who supported him in his long struggle with the book, understanding its importance.

"Don has been working on a different kind of poetry now that shows all his wisdom," she told me shortly after the book was done. By that time I had moved from New Hampshire to the University of Maine at Farmington, where I had invited her to read her poems. Walking together to a class for discussion of her work before the reading, she and I made quite a pair: I was depressed about a long poem in progress that wasn't working out, and she, worse off, had undergone a period of clinical depression. "I haven't been feeling well for a long time," she told me. "The poems of the book I've just finished are very melancholy, very dark," she added, shaking her head and pressing her lips together as she always did when she was distressed. "You'll see when I read them tonight."

At the reading some of the poems from the new book, *Let Evening Come,* seemed to have their own wisdom, suggesting that while her husband had been working on the poetry she praised for being wise, she had been expanding the brief lyric to include a wisdom of her own. One of these was "The Pear":

> There is a moment in middle age
> when you grow bored, angered

by your middling mind,
afraid.

That day the sun
burns hot and bright,
making you more desolate.

It happens subtly, as when a pear
spoils from the inside out,
and you may not be aware
until things have gone too far.

There were other new variations in the work of *Let Evening Come,* clearer to me as I read it now, six years later. The associations of certain poems—some imitating the form of notes and letters, others involving vignettes and thoughts about travel—were more complex. Moreover, in poems like "On the Aisle" and "At the Public Market Museum: Charleston, South Carolina," Kenyon had begun to deal with concerns in the world outside of her inner struggles. Finally, there were hints in her handling of narration of the deepening influence of Chekhov, and a new, Bishop-like way of addressing the reader as a confidante.

Yet just as she had warned, the poems also had a great sorrow in them—a sorrow also evident in *The Boat of Quiet Hours* and her fourth collection, *Constance.* Notwithstanding their moments of lightness and their moving mysticism, all of these books contain themes of terminal illness and death, depression, detachment from the body, and alienation from social life. All reach back to a childhood troubled by psychological stress and the misunderstanding of others. Their narrators often speak with a child's innocence, too, offering the disturbance they feel so calmly and simply, the poems are the more unsettling as we ponder them. A friend who knew Kenyon once told me that when she asked the poet to describe her process of writing, Kenyon told her it was always "gut-wrenching." Given the dark content of the poems and Kenyon's attempt in many of them to deal with extreme personal difficulties, this description is not hard to believe. It seems likely to me that the enormous stability and understanding she found in her relationship with Hall helped her to persist with such difficult subject matter.

But she got even more help from her remarkable determination—what Hall termed her "example of overcoming obstacles, personal and emotional ones." That determination is never more clearly seen than in *Constance*, where, in addition to returning to the subject of her father's death, first taken up in *The Boat of Quiet Hours*, she confronted the most serious personal and emotional obstacles she ever experienced: her lifelong depression and her fear of Donald Hall's cancer. The result was some of her most poignant poems—"Chrysanthemums," the nine-part "Having It Out with Melancholy," and "Pharoah." One can only imagine how difficult it was for Kenyon to write the concluding stanza of "Pharoah," conceding, as it does, the possibility of Hall's death:

> I woke in the night to see your
> diminished bulk lying beside me—
> you on your back, like a sarcophagus
> as your feet held up the covers. . . .
> The things you might need in the next
> life surrounded you—your comb and glasses,
> water, a book and a pen.

In the meantime, Hall continued to write about Kenyon, this time in *The Museum of Clear Ideas*, which was released in the same year *Constance* was published. In some of the sections of Hall's title poem, he attempts to quiet Kenyon's anxiety about him, giving a reader of the two books the odd and moving impression of a dialogue taking place between the two poets, across volumes. The most affecting example is "Mount Kearsarge Shines," where the speaker uses images of weather to discuss with "Camilla" (Kenyon's name in the title poem) the possible recurrence of his cancer and to qualify its threat:

Storms stop when they stop, no sooner,
leaving the birches glossy

with ice and bent glittering to rimy ground.
We'll avoid the programmed weatherman grinning
from the box, cheerful with tempest,
and take the day as it comes,

one day at a time, the way everyone says.
These hours are the best because we hold them close
in our uxorious nation.
Soon we'll walk—when days turn fair

and frost stays off—over old roads, listening
for peepers as spring comes on, never to miss
the day's offering of pleasure
for the government of two.

As it was in *The One Day*, the relationship between Hall
and Kenyon is extremely important to Hall's title poem in
The Museum of Clear Ideas; for the stability of that relationship
helps the poem's narrator to stand apart from the world in
which he lives and to view it with distance and clarity. Yet our
awareness of what his precarious health might do to the "gov-
ernment of two" threatens the equanimity of the speaker's
vision, occasionally jiggling the lens. Thus, the same Camilla
sections that help the narrator achieve his distance also sug-
gest a vulnerability and humanity that temper his remoteness,
making the view he offers easier to accept.

But alas, we live in a world where governments fail and
nations disappear, sometimes in the least predictable ways; it
was Jane Kenyon, not Donald Hall, who got the cancer, and
she who died of it. I remember going to dinner with them
just after Christmas in New Hampshire, where the three of us
exchanged and signed volumes of poetry, each having pub-
lished one earlier in the year. I recall, too, the apprehension
just beneath our festivity about Hall's health. So when I re-

ceived a note Hall sent us less than two months later, I was shocked to read its news of Kenyon's leukemia.

During her illness and their attempts to cure it through a bone-marrow transplant operation, Hall worked to complete a new book—his twelfth volume, *The Old Life*—which bears more of Kenyon's influence than ever. Like every collection Hall ever wrote after his marriage to Kenyon, this one is dedicated to her and includes, among other poems, verse about their life together. But unlike the other volumes, *The Old Life*, a poem in eighty-odd parts, contains a series of brief lyrics that closely resemble Kenyon's in their form, the images and events of each gathering toward a concluding disclosure or epiphany. As in Kenyon, Hall's disclosure sometimes comes by surprise out of events that predicted it all along:

> We walked in the white house
> like ghosts among ghosts who cherished us.
>   Everything we looked at
> exalted and raptured our spirits:—
>   full moon, pale blue
> asters, swamp maples Chinese red, ghost birches,
>   stone walls, cellar holes,
> and lopsided stretched farmhouses like ours.
>   The old tenants watched us
> settle in, five years, and then the house
>   shifted on its two-hundred-
> year-old sills, and became our house.

Sometimes the concluding disclosure is less predictable, as in this lyric about Kenyon's depressions:

> Curled on the sofa
> in the fetal position, Jane wept day
>   and night, night and day.
> I could not touch her; I could do nothing.
>   Melancholia fell

> like rain over Ireland for weeks
> without end.
> I never
> belittled her sorrows or joshed at
> her dreads and miseries.
> How admirable I found myself.

However the conclusion is handled, the result is the sudden twist Kenyon admired in the poems of Akhmatova.

In the days just before Kenyon's death, the two worked to assemble her last volume *Otherwise*, a collection of new and selected verse. The book's new poems were among the best she had ever done, striking in their variety and their coherence. Continuing to explore the short lyric (the majority of the poems were half a page long or less), she dealt with dark themes familiar from earlier books— her father's dying and Hall's cancer—adding poems about the death of her mother-in-law. Yet there was a new range of emotional tone, which included both sorrow and happiness, "Happiness" being, in fact, the title of one of the poems. Moreover, Kenyon was less tied to autobiographical detail, exercising a new freedom of invention, and using the third person to deal with events and issues in the world around her. Finally, there was a new integration of religious belief and poetic observation, showing us how strongly faith guided Kenyon and shaped her view of the world.

Of this last work, the only poem written during Kenyon's illness was "The Sick Wife," on which, as Hall says in his afterword to *Otherwise*, she "would have made more changes if she had lived." This poem features Kenyon and Hall, as many earlier ones do. Yet while the earlier pieces are often love poems, "The Sick Wife" speaks of love's absence. Since the husband of the piece has gone for groceries, the wife, helpless in her illness, is left to watch "even the old and relatively infirm" move outside in the parking lot and the cars alongside of her pull "away so briskly/ that it [makes] her sick at heart." Whereas the Kenyon of the earlier poems is at home in the place where love and work happen, the sick wife is in all ways displaced, neither at home, nor able to join the world's traffic. Choosing the third person to portray the wife in this poem, Kenyon stands eerily outside of herself, observing not only the verse's moment but her own finite history.

Yet in spite of "The Sick Wife" the love poems about Kenyon and Hall continue, because in his grief, Donald Hall goes on writing about his mate, and even—in the concluding poems of his current volume *Without*—to her. In an interview on the NPR program *Fresh Air* done while he was completing *Without,* Hall declared that everything he had done as a poet seemed to him a preparation for the poetry he is now involved with. Then he read a sample, "Weeds and Peonies," one of his most beautiful elegies, where he paces between the weedy garden Kenyon left behind and her newly blossoming peonies by the porch of the ancestral farmhouse. Watching their petals blow across the abandoned garden, he imagines Kenyon vanishing into snowflakes; looking up at Mount Kearsarge, he thinks of the words he spoke when she went off for a day of climbing: "Hurry back"—words that are useless now. Hall's elegy is the more poignant for the way it interweaves words and images from Kenyon's poems, as if to illustrate the interdependency that sustained the two poets in their life together. There are references to Kenyon's walking with Gus, the dog that appears in her third and fourth volumes, and to snowflakes as particles, a metaphor used first in her poem "Winter Lambs." Describing the peonies, a favorite subject in Kenyon's work, Hall uses the words "prodigies," "heads," and "topple"—all found in earlier Kenyon poems and releasing a range of sorrowful meanings best appreciated by studying the original sources and the new context Hall's elegy has provided. In one of its lines "Weeds and Peonies" even refers to a poem Hall included in his first New Hampshire book, "Old Roses"—a love poem to Kenyon which spoke of the beauty of the old roses around the Wilmot farmhouse and, ironically, how quickly they perish.

No doubt this allusive and moving poem, and the interview during which Donald Hall read it, will continue to spread the legendary story of two poets, drawing readers to the work of Hall and Kenyon, and at the same time distorting that work and making it more difficult to assess. But there will be time in the future for such assessments. For now, we may simply be grateful for the abundance of poetry these two have written over the last twenty-five years—poems both local and universal in their subjects, which range from despair to celebration. And we may give thanks for the unique relationship that brought such poetry to us.

Boothed

When I was just beginning to find the poems of Philip Booth in the early 70s, I read a collection by Robert Creeley, and with Creeley's lines and speech in my head, wrote the following for the amusement of fellow literature teachers at my New Hampshire college.

> Robert Creeley
> eats peanut butter
> sandwiches,
>
> though Robt
> would say
> 'peanut buttr,'
>
> which is
> profoundr.

*

This parody, its abbreviations inspired by Creeley's famous poem "I Know a Man," suggests the trouble I had not only with the abstraction of his poetry, but with the importance his short lines sometimes gave to words and phrases that were, to my eye, slighter than he assumed. I understand now that in spite of my parody, I was attracted even then to the way Creeley made the space around his lines and stanzas—that wordless otherness—part of what he was saying, so that his complicated, Jamesian sentences took on a kind of philosophical spaciness as they moved slowly down the page. Still, when it came to the short lines of free verse, I was more attracted to Booth. He was, for one thing, a lot closer to the ground. In her famous poem "Poetry," Marianne Moore favored poets who were "literalists of the imagination." Philip Booth, assigning each detail, fact and word with the greatest precision, is one of imagination's literalists.

HARD COUNTRY

In hard
country each white
house, separated
by granite outcrop
from each white
house pitches
its roofline
against the hard sky.
Hand-split
shakes, fillet
and face plank, clap-
board, flashing
and lintel: every
fit part over-
laps from the ridge
board on down, wind-
tight, down
to the sideyard back
door, shut against
eavesdrop. . .

*

Shortly after I arrived at Colby-Sawyer College, I was introduced to Booth's work through a poem everyone in the composition program taught, "Siasconset Song." My single-sex college tended to attract privileged young women whose values were often other-directed and materialistic; the poem offered the chance to discuss the limits of those values and the importance of cultivating deeper ones.

SIASCONSET SONG

The girls
of golden summers whirl
through sunsprung
bright Julys
with born right
sky-bright
star-night
eyes;

everywhere
their tennis-twirl
of young gold
legs and arms,
they singsong
summer-long
I-belong
charms;

and through
the summer sailing whirl
they cut like
shining knives
in sun-told
never old
ever gold
lives.

Rediscovering this poem in *Letters to a Distant Land*, Booth's first book, I now notice how it departs from the rhyme and meter of other early poems, on its way to the free verse of his later work. Yet the poem improvises its own system of rhythm, its own repetitions of sound. Booth once remarked to Richard Jackson in an interview that unless he heard "the rhythm in the words, the poem [was] bound to go wrong;" in another interview, done with Stephen Dunn, he stressed the importance of "recurrence." The musical recursions of "Siasconset Song" show his departure from techniques he never—here or in later work—quite leaves behind.

*

"Why didn't you include 'Siasconset Song' in your last *Selected?*" I recently asked him in a note. It was an early poem, he wrote back, that now seemed to him "slightly stylish." Compelled by what he said about the piece in his neatly typed postcard, I was even more compelled by how he said it, beginning with his opening sentence, whose diction was pure Booth in its staccato rhythm and its process of statement and qualification, the work of six verbs. "I didn't, and don't, seem to feel (or think) that *that* poem is worthy of any *Selected*," he said. I heard and saw:

> I didn't
> and don't seem
> to feel
>
> (or think)
> that *that*
> poem is worthy
>
> of any
> *Selected.*

Printed in this way, the sentence resembles not only a Booth poem, but how—as I learned when I finally met him—Booth talks: phrase by phrase, punctuating with shifts of tone and emphasis.

*

Teaching "Siasconset Song" had led me to search out more Booth in the college library, where I discovered *Letter to a Distant Land* and other verses with short lines. Later on, I found his well-known piece "Hard Country," in an anthology. These poems, together with work by William Carlos Williams and the poems by Robert Creeley I thought I didn't like, helped me to write my own short lines in free verse. Thinking back on approaches my readings taught me, I think especially of the poems of Booth.

*

Approach 1. While the long line in free verse, giving full access to the sentence, says, "This is all I think, this is all there is," the short line says, "There's something else, there's something more," and it is meant for qualification, anticipation, and mystery. Here is Booth's "A Late Spring: Eastport":

> On the far side
> of the storm
> window, as close
>
> as a tree
> might grow to
> a house,
>
> beads of rain
> hang cold
> on the lilac . . .

*

2. Stripping the sentence down to one fragment after another as in "A Late Spring: Eastport," the short line undertakes a kind of reduction, yet through that very process increases the sentence's complexity and meaning. Poetry's old strategy: out of compression, enlargement.

*

3. The poem in short lines is a scrupulous record of a process of thought. Twists and turns in the process make the poem more engaging.

A SLOW BREAKER

> Washing on granite
> before it turns
> on itself, away

from every horizon
it fetched from,
this clear green wash,

the flashing, cold,
specific gravity of it,
calls the eye down

to what we thought to
look into, to all we
cannot see through.

4. The tension between short lines and long sentences can help to create feeling and make it grow until the poem seems barely able to contain it. "Panic" provides a model:

It is to be out
of familiar walls
with no place left
but the Halfway
House far up
the block: it is
this first after-
noon, to carefully
ask your new self
for a walk beyond
the drugstore around
the block, but then
to have to refuse;
it is to remember
how trees grow out
of the sidewalk, to
figure how this time
to face him: the one
with hair like old vines
who steps out of
nowhere, trying to
take you over, back
where he always
comes from; it is

having moved here
instead: here to
sleep, to learn
to get up; it is,
at supper the always
first night, to
try to ask for
the salt. And having it
passed, it's to weep.

*

5. Or consider how the speaker himself may be contained
in a short-line poem, as in Booth's "Word," whose narrator
explores his sentences, line by line, coming back to words and
phrases as if he were in a room with a secret door and feeling
the walls for the way out, the right passage for his passage.

In a flat month
in a low field

I hit on a word
with just one

meaning. One.
It got to me,

hard. I stood
back up, grabbing

for balance; I
tried to hit

back. But it
meant it: no

matter what I
did, nothing

would yield . . .

*

Taking instruction from the compressed poems of Philip Booth, one cannot avoid the theme of containment for long, or resist seeing the poem as a kind of container or compartment—a booth. Among visual artists, a sure relative is Cornell. For the booth of a Booth poem is a Cornell-like enclosure, its arrangement of words, phrases and stanzas a puzzle of the deconstructed sentence that we must, by applying mind and feeling, put together.

*

In fact, the deconstructed sentences of Philip Booth have ancestors among free verse's earliest poems—for instance, those tiny Cubist productions of William Carlos Williams like "Poem," where the cat appears whole and in various pieces as he moves, line by broken line:

> As the cat
> steps over
> the top of
>
> the jamcloset
> first the right
> forefoot
>
> carefully
> then the hind
> stepped down
>
> into the pit of
> the empty
> flowerpot.

*

It is no wonder that in a tribute to W.C. Williams, Philip Booth remarks about his syntax. In "Poem" the single sentence builds, picking up observations as it goes and holding them in suspension until at last the sentence breaks, its main verb "stepped" carrying cat, observations and all to the swift conclusion of the last stanza. In his tribute Booth also mentions Williams' "measure," a term referring to the shape and pacing of the Williams line. Finding this word in my rereading of his essay, I notice not only its relation to music, but to its counting.

*

In "Adding It Up," Booth writes,

> I'm Puritan to the bone, down to
> the marrow and then some:
> if I'm not sorry I worry,
> if I can't worry I count.

Oddly enough, the very thing I was once intrigued by in his early work—his literalist tendency—I now resist, sensing that the impulse in his work to count, verify, qualify, and transcribe pre-empts the impulse to transform.

*

For John Keats, the transformation poetry requires depends utterly on the heart, the "hornbook" of life's schoolroom. For Philip Booth, confessed Puritan, the heart has not always been so easy to open—pointing up the dangers of the short line, which may afford too much control over the sentence; may give too much to turns of wit and wordplay; may use form to justify caution; may strip too much away, leaving feeling itself out. Was it feeling Booth meant when in his interview with Stephen Dunn he said that "too much was kept out of the poem"?

*

In his upstairs study hearing him read his poems for the first time, I find a Philip Booth of great feeling. The moment means enough to me that when I recall it, I am immediately with him in that room. It is late fall, 1992, the day after I have read my poetry near his home in Blue Hill, to an audience that has included him and his wife Margaret, and by his generous arrangement, I have stayed overnight at his house. The poem he now reads to me, this man who seldom gives public readings, is a new poem, planned for his new book. His face is intent, expressive; his voice, earnest. In the inflection he gives to each word, Philip Booth reaches out beyond any reserve. One sees in him—feels in him—how much this poem matters; how much poetry matters.

Before we go back downstairs, Philip Booth shows me his notebook of submissions to magazines, an intricate gridwork of checkmarks and notations providing a detailed record of each poem: where it has been sent, and when, and how long the process of submission has taken.

*

Then we travel in his Toyota, damaged from a small accident, around Castine—first to the insurance man for an estimate of how much it will cost to fix the car, then to the place where his mentor and friend Robert Lowell summered, then on to a detailed tour of the town and its inhabitants. I remember the opening of his poem "Small Town":

> You know.
> The light on upstairs
> before four every morning. The man
> asleep every night before eight.
> What programs they watch. Who
> traded cars, what keeps the town
> moving . . .

*

And the whole time, somewhere in my head, are those short, often enjambed lines which Philip Booth has employed to translate this place on the sea: the rhythms of its worklife, for instance, in poems such as "Dragging"; the laconic and understated speech of its Downeast natives; the skills of sailing he learned here—a direct influence on his poetry, as this remark from his interview with Stephen Dunn shows:

> . . . I think there is a resistance [in the use of words] that is more like the resistance of sailing to windward and having to tack by necessity as the wind changes slightly. There is a kind of prosody . . . which allows one to sail with beautiful freedoms with a closed course.

But most of all as we tour Castine, I think of his fathers in creative expression—not the literary ones, such as Thoreau, a figure in his poetry early and late, but his painterly fathers, whose pictures portrayed his Maine coast. John Marin, celebrated in Booth's poem "Sea-Change," is one, a painter whose approach is, like Booth's, suggestive and poetic, and who is an inveterate framer, often adding to the picture-frame up to three additional frames applied by paint—as Booth adds to the structure of line and regular stanza a carefully structured language, frames within the frame. Even more, I think of Fitz Hugh Lane, the nineteenth-century painter of Castine and Blue Hill. Painstaking, like Booth, in matters of detail, scale, and arrangement, he transformed the very coast we looked out upon into Transcendental visions of light.

*

The night before as Philip Booth, his wife Margaret and I talk in their living room, he speaks of another father, Robert Frost. Not only speaks *of*, but speaks *as*. His impression is more Frost than Frost. But then, he has heard Frost speak oftener than most, first as his student at Dartmouth, and later on, when Booth was teaching at Wellesley, in Cambridge. There, he was sometimes charged by Kathleen Morrison to take Frost home from readings so he would be home by 12:00 a.m. On one such midnight occasion, Frost told him, "We'd better go home now, or Kay won't trust you to do this again," but when Booth arrived at Frost's house, the elder poet sat in the car and talked, unwilling to go alone into the dark.

There are other Frost stories. When Booth was a U.S. Army Air Corps trainee during World War II, Frost purchased and inscribed his 1943 volume *Come In* so Booth's father could send it to him. Meeting with Booth after his return from the service, Frost asked him, "Did you kill anybody?" And learning Booth would soon marry a woman from Georgia whose father was a county sheriff, Frost wanted to know, "Did he ever shoot anybody?" Afterward, pondering Booth's flawless impression of Frost in all of his stories, I consider Frost's influence on Booth's poetic voice, how Booth's wry humor and his entanglement of grammar in unfolding sentences resemble Frost's.

*

All day after my visit I am Boothed. I think again of his house—likened, he told me, by Constance Hunting to his poetry in that its main entry is at the side. I think, too, of the distinction he made during our tour of Castine between "stuttering" and "stammering"—the one thing showing a disjunction of thought, the other showing the pressure of joining one thought to another—and I ponder the way Booth himself sometimes stammers on his way to the next phrase, not only in his talk, but in his poetry:

. . . Not to get it said

and be done, but to
say the feeling, its
present shape, to

let words lend it
dimension: to name
the pain to confirm

how it may be borne:
through what in
ourselves we dream

to give voice to,
to find some word for
how we bear our lives . . .

(SAYING IT)

*

Philip Booth says in the Dunn interview the poems he
has written that continue to satisfy him "are very few," add-
ing: "that they're there at all amazes me." What I find amaz-
ing is that Booth, now in his eighth decade, keeps writing
poems that satisfy, as in his recent collection *Selves*, where the
feeling is deeper than ever. My own favorite in that book is
"Presence," a poem praising life and the natural world. Put-
ting short lines aside, he uses long ones for "Presence";
whereas his less characteristic long-lined poems are continu-
ously enjambed, this verse combines enjambment with end-
stopping, giving the line an unusual freedom as it shapes the
poem's long sentences. The result is a Whitmanesque inclu-
siveness that is wholly remarkable: Booth unboothed.

PRESENCE

That we are here: that we can question who
we are, where; that we relate to how deer

once small have grown bold in our back garden;
that we can ask, ask even ourselves, how

to the other we may appear, here in the always near place
we seem to ourselves to inhabit, who sleep toward

and wake from steeped hills, the sea opening into our eyes
the infinite possibility of infinity

we believe we're neither beyond nor shy of,
here as we are, without doubt, amid then, there

and now, falling through dark into light, and back,
against which we cannot defend, wish as we might, as we do.

Still, as the physicist said, *the mystery is*
that we are here, here at all, still bearing with,

and borne by, all we try to make sense of:
this evening two does and a fawn who browse

the head lettuce we once thought was ours.
But no. As we chase them off mildly, and make

an odd salad of what they left us, the old stars
come casually out, and we see near and far we own nothing:

it's us who belong to all else; who, given this day,
are touched by, and touch, our tenderest knowing,

our lives incalculably dear as we feel for each other,
our skin no more or less thin than that of the redwing,

rainbow, star-nose, or whitethroat, enfolded like us
in the valleys and waves of this irrefutable planet.

*

Despite "Presence" and his other forays into the long
line, we are blessed that this poet has never been unboothed
for long, his short lines have brought us such pleasure—their
fragments of language the riddle we must solve as we read,
groping from line-break to line-break, thinking by touch. For
how, without those fragments that render the world we once
knew strange to our eyes, could we come to know the world
of Philip Booth, which he has spent more than a half-century
to create? To them, we owe the knowledge and wisdom this
poet has given us; to them, I owe a sense of my craft, this
hand-made boat that I now sail as a poet, seeking freedoms
within a course I have chosen, alert to all weathers.

Talking about Vermont
HAYDEN CARRUTH'S POETIC VOICE

Though the fact seems odd to me now, I did not come to know Hayden Carruth's verse until a few years ago. Had I known it earlier, particularly his Vermont poems, I would have found an ally in my struggle to bring the New England I knew into poetry. I would also have found a superb model for developing a poetic voice. In my view, the use of voice is Carruth's most distinctive technical achievement. No American poet since Eliot has explored voice as fully as he has. In addition to all the ways he speaks in his own persona—Carruth the elegist, storyteller, polemicist, and so on—there are his dramatic monologues in a range of American voices, from northern New England Yankees to urban blacks. In one book alone, *Asphalt Georgics,* he takes on the identities of over a dozen narrators who inhabit the cities and towns to the east and west of Syracuse, New York.

Yet what moves me most is not the diversity of voices in Carruth's poetry, but a single, characteristic way of speaking, which I hear in a characteristic poem. The poem I am thinking of is a kind of meditation, which in the classic sense, as defined by Louis L. Martz, is "an interior drama" featuring a persona who "projects a self upon a mental stage, and there comes to understand that self in the light of a divine presence." Of course, the presence we feel at the end of Carruth's version of the meditation is not exactly divine, though our awareness of self has, in one way or another, been heightened. Carruth departs from Martz's archetype again by mixing forms, so that what may appear to be a narrative poem about a country character, as in the case of his famous verse

"Marshall Washer," turns out also to be a reflection on the fate of traditional values in a world of materialism and change—or a poem like "All Things," quoted below, is simultaneously a lyric and a meditation about the meaning of song.

> The music of October
> is the wild geese in the night
> that bring me to rediscover
> above the citylight
>
> how all things are a song
> unmeaning but profound
> and fundamental to the tongue
> we speak here on the ground.
>
> St. Harmonie, let me sing
> the music of October
> in my loquacious stammering
> till all hell freezes over.

Even in this small verse, I begin to hear Carruth's characteristic way of speaking—first in the poem's plainspoken quality that preserves it from literariness in spite of its formalism, then in the last line, whose familiar Americanness and humor gently mocks the speaker's intensity at the same time it welcomes the reader into the poem to share the speaker's musings. To put it another way, we sense in the last line—the last stanza, in fact, with its droll juxtaposition of St. Harmonie and hell—that the narrator is speaking not so much to his saint as to us. The result is the companionability critics like Richard Tillinghast find in his work. "Something Hayden Carruth does as well as any living writer," Tillinghast notes, "is to treat the reader as a friend, and to provide, through his poetry, hours of good company." The element of companionability in Carruth's voice, well established by the late 1980's, is what makes books like *Sonnets* (1989) *Tell Me Again How the White Heron Rises and Flies Across the Nacreous River at Twilight toward the Distant Islands* (1989), *New Poems* (1991), and the recent *Scrambled Eggs and Whiskey* (1996) a pleasure to read for all their depth and complexity. A recent example of this poetry, the modest and lovely "Isabel's Garden, May 14," from *Scrambled Eggs and Whiskey,* is typical of how he talks to the reader. In this poem he introduces his speaker as a character, another typical approach.

The fruit trees are in full bloom.
Apple, crabapple, the dogwood tree
at work on its small inedible berry.
It's a flowering above eye-level, a warm
iridescent mist, beneath which the tulips
have begun to fall, their heads tousled
and frowsy; and elsewhere are
forget-me-nots, bluets, the first verbenas,
spreading patches of grape hyacinths,
rock pinks, a few white trilliums,
and other flowers, exotic beauties
from the seed catalogues—Isabel knows
their names but I can never remember.
Isabel is slender and beautiful and today
she is gardening in a pale blue blouse
and a long dark blue flowered skirt
with earrings and a necklace and lipstick.
She says she felt low this morning, so
she dressed up to work in her garden,
which is characteristic and perfectly sincere.
She looks as elegant as her flowers,
a companion to them. And what am
I, an old man on the porch peering
out at the world with a portable
computer on his lap, his scant hairs
tousled too, hands spotted and stiff,
brain hurting from too much drink
last night? And what is this poem—is it
necessity or an exercise? I am too old
to think about this any more. The poem
has grown on this screen like a flower,
letter by letter, cell by cell, color by

color, assuming its own brief
identity in the efflorescence. I am
the inelegant gardener soiling my
hands in the humus of the alphabet.

For Wendell Berry, Carruth's unusual relationship with
his reader derives from the honesty with which he speaks to
him. "In his poems," Berry says, "mind and heart speak as
one, and his work has, in rare degree, the quality of trustwor-
thiness." The openness Berry refers to is especially evident in
"Isabel's Garden, May 14," where we feel as though we our-
selves are being trusted with an intimate process of thought,
taken into the narrator's confidence line by line. That open-
ness contributes to the companionability of Carruth's best
and most characteristic work, which also conveys through
varied combinations of humor, compassion, and worldly un-
derstanding, a sense of the speaker's humanity.

Where does Hayden Carruth's unique way of speaking
in poetry come from? Its true development, I think, occurs in
his Vermont poems—particularly those of *From Snow and Rock,
From Chaos* and *Brothers, I Loved You All.* Before the Vermont
poems, Carruth's writing was often as James Dickey portrayed
it in his 1960 review of *The Crow and the Heart:* uneven verse,
at its worst "mechanical and lifeless, with more than a hint of
academic dilettantism." Nobody has been more critical of
those early poems than Carruth himself, who declared in the
final poem of his best-known Vermont collection, *Brothers, I
Loved You All,* that they were replete with "modes, names,
manners." In disgust Carruth asks, "What true voice?" and
follows his question with a description of past failures and a
self-challenge:

> . . . Humiliated, in throes
> of vacillation, roundhead to cavalier to ivy
> league to smartass—
> never who I was. Say it plain . . .

To grasp how the poems Hayden Carruth wrote in Vermont changed his poetry, making him sound like "who I was," one must first understand the personal changes he was going through as he made his life there. He arrived in the state settling with his wife in the town of Johnson after a nervous breakdown and confinement in a mental hospital. During a recent interview, Carruth told Mike Pride, "It took me years and years before I could walk from one end of the town to the other in Johnson, from the post office to the bank," adding that he had one purpose in his new rural location: "the remaking of myself . . . in order to overcome psychotic difficulties." Starting over as a farmer's helper and mechanic, far from the fast track of the publishing industry he had left behind in Chicago and New York, was central to his remaking. Without question, the poetry he wrote in Johnson played a part as well. Through it, he interpreted the meaning of his Vermont experience; through it, he was able to find his place in the deepest sense.

From Snow and Rock, From Chaos, the first collection dominated by Vermont, suggests that his psychotic difficulties were matched by the hardships of the life he chose. Winter is the book's primary season, and there is much darkness and bad weather. Whereas "that idiot Thoreau," as Carruth calls him in the poem "Concerning Necessity," released his spirit by hoeing in his New England bean field, Carruth's work in the poem leads only to chaos: a house "falling to pieces" and a car "coming apart." Chaos is also in the winter winds of "If It Were Not For You," which reach

> like the blind breath of the world
> in a rhythm without mind, gusting and beating
> as if to destroy us, battering our poverty
> and all the land's flat and cold and dark
> under the iron snow

As this passage implies, the disorder of Carruth's Vermont in *From Rock* reflects disorder and violence in the larger world. So while he wanders through frost-blighted woods in "This Song" and pushes aside pine branches, he feels "September's little knives" and thinks of the "violent times" in places beyond Vermont. And in "I Know, I Remember, But How Can I Help Him" northern lights suggest "other light-storms/ cold memories discursive and philosophical/ in my mind's burden." "The Birds of Vietnam" makes violence more explicit. There, he mourns the deaths of the birds poisoned and starved by warfare in Vietnam, and thinks of the endangered species that have been "harried, murdered, driven away" in his own state and nation.

How can the speaker of *From Rock and Snow, From Chaos* achieve wholeness in this place, threatened by natural forces and haunted by somber events? The answer is, through his love for his wife and ally. Over and over in the book he speaks to her in love poems whose feeling sustains and shelters him. It is in these poems – all written against a sense of dark alternatives—that Carruth's journey toward his characteristic voice begins.

One of them is "If It Were Not for You," quoted above, where love safeguards the narrator against the wild wind.

> Liebe, the world is wild
> and without intention
>
> how far
> this might be from the night of Christmas
> if it were not for you.

Deeply sympathetic to the loved one he addresses, the speaker is nonetheless candid about their difficult situation:

> Liebe, our light rekindled . . .
> in this dark of the blue mountain where only
> the winds gather
> is what we are for the time that we are
> what we know for the time that we know

How gravely and sweetly the poor touch in the
dark

In "The Decoration," addressed to his loved one, the
narrator recalls the ornament she made for him out of dis-
cards—dried flowers, pine-cone scales, and petals of maple
seed inside the cap of a cottage cheese carton—as if to show
how on their farm falling to pieces love can provide order.
The poem's short lines indicate the care and intimacy with
which he responds to her gift.

> . . . Beautiful
> flowers, unrecognizable
>
> flowers, at which I stare
> with a blue-green feeling,
> delighted and ignorant.
>
> until you tell me you
> made them up . . .

The emotion of "The Decoration," like that of "If It Were
Not for You" and other similar poems in *From Rock*, is the
more affecting because it takes place in the context of a shared
struggle. Sympathetic, confidential, and honest, the poem's
tone of voice says, "We are equals, you and I, in it together.
Let me tell you about this thing that has worried me, or this
thing that has delighted me." It is a voice that Carruth gradu-
ally adopts for much other poetry after *From Rock*, addressing
the reader in general, often speaking as a character.

Carruth rehearses not only a particular tone of voice in
his crucial book *From Rock*, but ways of talking in poetry, an
interest evident in earlier poems, which here gets special play.
The following phrases taken from a range of poems indicate
his preoccupation with spoken language; most also employ
the conversational mode of direct address, common to the
love poems.

. . . how come
they were so hot
to put the cold bones . . .

in this or another
remembered spot?

(FRENCH HILL)

The insomniac sleeps well for once and
rises at five, just when a late moon
rises . . .

You'll sleep ten hours if we let you . . .

(THE INSOMNIAC SLEEPS WELL FOR ONCE AND)

. . . Our absense
was spooked somehow; changes in spite of us . . .

. . . The pine stood shining
in snow when we last saw it, but the rust

took it . . .

(HOMECOMING)

You tourist, composed upon that fence . . . all I ask
is that when you go home you take
a close-up among your color slides
of vacationland, to show we pay the price
for hay . . .

(THE BALER)

In two of *From Rock* 's best poems, "The Cows at Night"
and "Emergency Haying," both of them meditations, Carruth
uses the sentence as we often use it in earnest conversation,
opening its syntax to the flow of thought and feeling. In such
conversation, there are breaks in the process of thought as a

speaker thinks and feels his sentence, stresses in meditation that we listen for, without knowing we do so, as evidence of his earnestness. The reverie of "The Cows at Night," with its shifts of time and place, and its long sentences that move across line breaks, shows how Carruth imitates the action of spoken thought. "Emergency Haying," too, moves as though it has been "talked out," containing loose, cumulative associations (involving haying, the slave laborers of Europe and Russia, and a newly risen moon), and featuring leaps of thought that seem nearly as surprising for the author as for the reader. In the poem's startling conclusion the narrator, standing with his sore arms stretched along the hayrack, imagines himself as Christ, warning the oppressors of men and women in the fields. His sudden alteration of voice as he assumes Christ's moral authority gives the poem a special power.

> . . . And who
> is the Christ now, who
>
> if not I? It must be so. My strength
> is legion. And I stand up high
> on the wagon tongue in my whole bones to say
>
> woe to you, watch out
> you sons of bitches who would drive men and women
> to the fields where they can only die.

Removing literary boundaries to speak directly and thoughtfully in their different ways, these two poems point the way to much of Carruth's future work, including that of *Brothers, I Loved You All.*

In *Brothers* the search for order and personal wholeness continues, and because Carruth's narrator in this book, like the one in *From Rock,* is haunted by thoughts of conflict, order is difficult to find. He imagines, in "The Mountain," a black man of an American city somewhere beyond his mountain carrying a submachine gun and engaged in combat that reminds him of the warfare he knew long before in Mussolini's Italy. Guns dominate other poems as well: "When Howitzers Began," for instance, with its scene of howitzers killing fish and "spreading . . . darkness over the river," and "Essay," which calls the current period in history "the time of the finishing off of animals." Nor can the narrator forget his past struggles with mental illness; so "That I Had Had Courage When Young" describes "the big lunatic house" where "I sat with madness in my mouth."

Yet the speaker in this book, like his earlier counterpart, discovers ways to free himself from his disturbing thoughts, ways that derive from Carruth's deepening knowledge of Vermont. In "The Loon at Forrester's Pond" he tells of his encounter with a loon, whose "insane song" reminds him of "the long wilderness" of his own life, haunted by madness. As he listens to the repetition of the loon's song—"the laugh" that is beyond mirth, sorrow, "and finally all knowledge"—he is taken out of his human self and made aware of a transcendent timelessness that becomes for him "the real and only sanity." Through his odd and comforting identification with the loon, the narrator gains a new sense of himself, as a man and as a poet with his own capacity for song.

That Carruth calls the loon "truly a vestige" is significant, since the nature that uplifts the narrator in *Brothers* – more benign than that of *From Rock* – is primordial, predating technology and the history of human exploitation. It is a nature represented by the moon in "The Joy and Agony of Improvisation," whose "color of old parchment" and "archaic" meaning can only be sensed by the poem's couple after they listen to the wild song the pines make in the night wind. And it is the nature that sings a song of love to the speaker's son in the forest, where the two of them walk as the narrator thinks of the slow "chaos" of technology which he, as a farmer with his own machines, has helped set in motion. Like the loon's song, the songs of the forest affirm both the deep harmony of nature, and the poet's authority as a singer inspired by the natural world.

Not only does the narrator of *Brothers* find alternatives
to disorder in nature, but in the love of his wife and son,
recorded by several of the book's poems. Yet even more im-
portant than those connections are the ones he finds with
neighbors in his Vermont community, to whom, in part,
Carruth refers in his book's title, devoting four of the volume's
longest poems to them. All independent individuals, they are
archaic vestiges themselves, associated in the poet's mind with
ancient agrarian traditions that continue despite the mod-
ern world's threat of chaos. More importantly for this essay,
they are the source for a significant expansion of Carruth's
poetic voice. For as he explains and demonstrates the value
of rural brotherhood in his four poems, his narrator takes on
the traditional dialect of the Vermonter himself, speaking to
the reader with a range of feeling, a humor and—for all of
his regionalisms—an Americanness that were not present in
his work before.

Carruth's new exploration of voice begins in his appre-
ciation of the tie between the old traditions of his neighbors'
speech and their ongoing customs of farming. Examining the
country expressions of his next-door neighbor and friend
Marshall Washer, he describes that link:

> He says "I didn't mind it" for "I didn't notice it,"
> "dreened" for "drained," "climb" (pronounced
> climm)
> for "climbed," "stanchel" for "stanchion,"
> and many other unfamiliar locutions; but I
> have looked them up, they are in the dictionary,
> standard speech of lost times. He is rooted
> in history as in the land, the only man I know
> who lives in the house where he was born. I see
> a man alone walking in his fields and woods,
> knowing every useful thing about them, moving
> in a texture of memory that sustains his lifetime
> and his father's lifetime . . .
>
> (MARSHALL WASHER)

An elegy that places Washer in the context of dying farms, this poem's tone is very different from the humorous one we find in "John Dryden." There, Carruth both transcribes and imitates the speech of a garrulous eccentric who occasionally works as a hired hand and lives by himself in the woods. The following passage illustrates the texture of conversation in the poem, written, as it is, in one long sentence that moves from point to point in the manner of Dryden's breathless talk.

> . . . there's plenty
> more he could tell you, like how he got bit that time
> by the cattle grub and took the "purple aguey,"
> or how he has a buckshot in him that keeps going
> round and round in his veins, catching him sharp-like
> on his cotterbone when he don't expect it
> every now and again, or how he eats forty aspirins
> a day and hears sweet patooty music in his ears,
> or how he fell in a cellarhole at blackberrying time
> and landed on a bear – "I says, 'Whuff, old bear,
> get you away from me,' and then I climm the hell
> out of there" – or how . . . but have you noticed
> I can't talk about him without talking like him?

In all of these poems, Carruth addresses us as a character who observes and adopts the speech of his neighbors. In "Lady," a dramatic monologue that is by turns humorous and serious, he enters the character of his neighbor, making her—speech, archaisms, country expressions and all—wholly his own. Here is a sample, Lady's description of an encounter with a bear:

> I whooped, let me tell you, and threw my fork
> and climm back on that tractor in a kind of a hurry,
> breathing a mite hard. And when I got back to the barn
> I found I had more manure than I started out with.

I told Jasper the next day. He owns that
gone-to-Boston-looking place over the hill
with the bam-o-gilly in the dooryard. "Jas,"
I says, "I was plain *scart*—scart of that old she bear.
I shit my britches." Jas, he looked straight and soft-like.
"Lady," he says, "I don't blame you none. 'Twas me
I believe I'd of shatten too.' "

Having embraced the language of his Vermont commu-
nity and assimilated it into his poetic voice, Carruth is pre-
pared for "Paragraphs," the long concluding poem of *Broth-
ers.* The poem is an attack against the despoilation of rural
Vermont by businessmen, developers, greedy farmers, and
the government. But it is also a declaration of the power of
poetic speech, in particular the speech of Hayden Carruth.
He is the Yankee "Appolyon" who enters the poem in the
dialect of a Vermonter, and who goes on not only to name
the purveyors of disorder in his state and nation, but to imag-
ine an alternative vision of human love and creativity. Carruth
is emboldened in his declaration not only by the faith his
fellow Vermonters have given him in what he calls "oldwords,"
but by the music of jazz, whose rousing clamor of tones pro-
vides the climactic moment of his vision:

. . . it was music
music now
with Ammons trilling in counterpoise.
Byas next, meditative, soft/
then Page
with that tone like the torn edge
of reality:

and so the climax, long dying riffs—
groans, wild with pain—
and Crosby throbbing *and* Catlett riding stiff
yet it was music   music . . .

What does jazz have to do with Hayden Carruth's voice as a poet? In his *Contemporary Authors* interview, he himself explains:

> Certainly one of the strongest influences on all my thinking and feeling about art has been jazz music. . . . The tonal and textural and syntactical qualities of jazz improvisation, and especially blues, I think have influenced my writing as much as anything else.

Exactly when and how jazz has affected Carruth's speech in his poems, a subtler interpreter than I would have to determine, though it is clear that as it flows line to line in his mature work, his voice often has, like the music performed by each of the players named above, the feel of an inspired riff. It is easier to explain, given his reference to blues in the above quotation, why he chose "Bottom Blues" as the song that lifts musicians and readers alike "high above themselves" at the end of "Paragraphs" to a new understanding of human possibility. Thus the theme of music in *Brothers* moves from the song of the Vermont forest and the loon to the music of Albert Ammons, Lips Page, Vic Dickenson, Don Byas, Israel Crosby, and Big Sid Catlett, Hayden Carruth's musical "brothers."

Perhaps the most remarkable thing about Carruth's book, seen among other collections of the late twentieth century, is that it ends in such triumph, celebrating the full arrival of his poetic voice at the same time it illustrates what "Paragraphs" calls the "glory of our human shining." Of course, that triumph also includes the remaking for which he came to Vermont in the first place, staying on to farm and write books like *From Rock and Snow, From Chaos* and *Brothers, I Loved You All.* For being remade as a poet in this final poem, Hayden Carruth is also remade as a man. "What true voice?" Carruth asks in the section of "Paragraphs" quoted at the outset of this essay, then claims for himself the motto that his journey as a poet has taught him: "Say it plain." No motto could be more appropriate for him, emphasizing, as it does, not only a direct and common language, but the possibilities that lie in speaking it.

The Triumph of Robert Francis

I suppose my favorite poem by New England poet Robert Francis is everyone's, it is so often anthologized. The poem's title is "The Pitcher," and it is classic Francis.

> His art is eccentricity, his aim
> How not to hit the mark he seems to aim at.
>
> His passion how to avoid the obvious.
> His technique how to vary the avoidance.
>
> The others throw to be comprehended. He
> throws to be a moment misunderstood.
>
> Yet not too much. Not errant, arrant, wild,
> But every seeming aberration willed.
>
> Not to, yet still, still to communicate
> Making the batter understand too late.

There is the characteristic wordplay of stanza four, for instance, and throughout "The Pitcher," the play of opposites so typical of Francis' work. Above all, there is the offbeat precision of the poem's form—its couplets setting off the paradoxical two's they contain, its movement toward rhyme culminating in the perfect rhyming of the last stanza, where the verse's perfect throw is completed.

The technique of Francis' poem offers so much to admire, we might not see at first (temporarily blinded, like the batter) that the pitcher is also a poet, and that what has gotten by us is a description of how the poet works. Look again at the pitcher's windup—its "eccentricity" and "willed aberration"—and we see the pitcher is very like Francis himself. For the poem not only presents pitcher and batter, but somewhere at the edges another couple, Robert Francis and his metaphor of the pitcher, through which he explores and affirms his own method as a poet.

In helping him to explore and affirm his craft, "The Pitcher," along with several other poems about art and the artist that Francis was working on in mid-career, had an incalculable value. The poems helped him to find his bearings during a period of rejection from editors and the literary world that had gone on so long he came to question whether he should continue as a poet. Recalling that time in his autobiography, *The Trouble with Francis*, he wrote:

> I wanted to crawl into a corner out of sight, I wanted to shrink into my psychic shell. Night after night, soon after supper, my house became dark and inhospitable, not a wink of light visible from the outside. . . . I was in hiding . . .

Eventually, Francis saw that the only way he could get out of his corner was to write himself out, a process that began with the poems about poetry and art, and ended with the best work of his career. The story of how Francis freed himself, overthrowing his mentor Robert Frost as he did so, is enough to encourage any aspiring poet.

In Francis' early journal entries, there is no trace of the despair that swept over him in his later life. Francis was just beginning a series of visits to the home of Robert Frost in Amherst, visits which included discussions of his own poetry, and his journal from that time is full of the excitement he felt at having Frost as a mentor. "I thought as I came away from the house that I had been given help of a kind and an authority that I could have perhaps received from no other man in America," he declared. And later: "When I left I told Mr. Frost he had given me enough to live on for the next five or six months. . . . No visit has done me more good."

In his journal Robert Francis took detailed notes on the methods which Robert Frost recommended. There was advice given about rhyme, and about factual accuracy. Francis was to be unliterary in his language ("people don't talk that way—it's arty," Frost told him about one of his early poems). Above all, Francis was to avoid the "precious and disdainful" approaches of the "Archibald MacLeish-T.S. Eliot gang." Formal, realistic, conversational, and accessible, the poetry Frost taught was exactly like his own.

Relying on Frost's advice, Francis wrote the poems of his first books—poems in what Francis was later to call his "relaxed traditional style." And while critics began to accuse Francis of imitating the older poet, he often extended the Frost aesthetic in these earlier verses, making it his. In "The Laughers," for instance, he opens with a conversational and humorous tone and moves to a concluding sentence that is surprisingly compressed, its enjambed lines leading swiftly to a dark conclusion.

> I drove an old man to a funeral
> And on the way he said, "What do they mean,
> These men who die at sixty, sixty-five?
> Here I am going on to seventy-two
> And hard at work. Of course my heart is bad
> And I have kidney stones, but otherwise—"
>
> I told my father and he laughed. He laughed
> Less than two years ago and I laughed with him.
> Now both of them—the laugher and the man
> We laughed about—have gone to where nobody
> (This is a joke my father would enjoy)
> Laughs, or if he does, nobody hears.

In "Old Roofs," a poem which depends on factual observation, Francis ends by suggesting that facts are not enough—that in order to know them, we must see through them to something larger. So the roofs of houses become geometry problems, challenging us to a fuller understanding.

Old roofs that only yesterday
Were dingy indiscriminate gray

With no appreciable design
And no one clean-cut slope or line

Now startle and delight the eye—
Clear white against the winter sky.

Their surfaces are all intact,
Their corners sharp, their lines exact

As if their purpose was to show
The plane geometry of snow.

They look like problems waiting proof—
Your roof, my roof, any old roof.

"Willow Woman," Frostian in its realism and accessibility, contains a portrait of a woman who offers pussy willows no one will buy. But on a less accessible level, the poem hints at the woman's alter ego, Robert Francis himself, who suffered the marketplace's indifference to his poems.

A woman with pinched fingers and pinched face
Is selling pussy willows on the street.
The buds are wearing something fine in fur.
A burlap rag is rug about her feet.

Nobody buys. Nobody stops for her.
Poor woman, willow woman, don't you know
It's only winter in the marketplace
However springlike where the willows grow?

By the time "Willow Woman" was published, Robert Francis had already felt the indifference of editors. The poem appeared in a volume Francis was forced to publish himself, after knocking, as he put it, "on the doors of New York and Boston in vain." A short time later that volume, *The Sound I*

Listened For, was reprinted by his old publisher, MacMillan, submitted there by an editor Francis met at the Bread Loaf School. However, the reprieve from rejection was shortlived. After 1944, when *The Sound* was released for the second time, he suffered a hiatus of 16 years during which he could not place a book of his poems and for long periods went without even magazine publication.

Francis' response to the rejection was to publish another volume by himself. "Yesterday," he declares in his journal entry for April, 1952, "I took the manuscript of my fourth volume of poems, *The Face Against the Glass,* to the printer Newell . . . to be a small paper-covered volume issued under my own auspices. Again I have cut the Gordian knot." In spite of the bravado, Francis had in that year reached what he later called "my low point." It was in 1952 that he spent many nights closed away in his bedroom, "a heavy drapery over its one window and a rug covering a crack in its one door," traumatized by the literary world's disregard. He questioned the value of his work, and he even questioned the judgment of his mentor Robert Frost, whose authority he had always accepted, even when critics had accused him of following the older poet too closely. "When Frost praises my work highly," he asked in his journal, "am I wise to accept the praise unqualifiedly? Am I wise to assume that he is right and all the other people who do not praise me are wrong?"

When Robert Francis at last returned to poetry, he did so with a new sense of ultimates, stripped of everything but his deep feeling for his vocation. "I am now trying to devote myself to poetry as unstintingly as mystic to God or as lover to beloved," he wrote in his journal.

> I am poor, I am unpublished, I am obscure. If I devote myself to what is most important . . . my poverty will not greatly trouble me, will perhaps not seem like failure at all. . . . Since the likelihood of winning any of the prizes is small, I might as well aim at the great targets.

As Francis took his new aim at poetry, he completed his several poems about art and the artist, exploring through them what he already knew, and what he needed to know for the further development of his craft. *The Orb Weaver*, the book which finally broke Francis' long period of rejection by book editors, contains eleven such poems. He wrote of the difficulties of including the world's variety in art ("Exclusive Blue") and of the difficulties of craftsmanship ("The Orb Weaver"). He considered the qualities of art that may be found in life even before the artist applies his skills ("Dry Point," "Tomatoes") and he pondered the trick of making art lifelike ("The Wrestlers").

The figure of the artist in *The Orb Weaver* has many disguises. He is the baseball pitcher in the poem that began this essay, and he is the "pure boy" of "Beyond Biology," caught in the act of peeing:

> Teased and titillated by the need
> Always of something more than necessary,
> Some by-product beyond biology,
> The poet is like a boy poised on a rock
> Who must produce an original waterfall,
> Father a brook, or fertilize a tree . . .

In "Waxwings" he is Robert Francis in the form of a cedar waxwing on a bush, chatting with four others of his kind:

> . . . Such merriment and such sobriety—
> the small wild fruit on the tall stalk—
> was this not always my true style?

In "Catch" the artist is again a boy, who with another boy plays toss and catch with a "poem." Are these two—instancing Francis' continous preoccupation with pairs—the imagining self and the writing self? The writer and the reader? However we interpret them and the game they play together, the poem they play with is very like the one Francis himself was developing in the late period of his verse: more various in its approach than his earlier work, bolder in its use of language, more challenging for the reader, and the author as well.

> Two boys uncoached are tossing a poem together,
> Overhand, underhand, backhand, sleight of hand,
>   every hand,
> Teasing with attitudes, latitudes, interludes, altitudes,
> High, make him fly off the ground for it, low, make
>   him stoop,
> Make him scoop it up, make him as-almost-as-possible
>   miss it,
> Fast, let him sting from it, now, now fool him slowly,
> Anything, everything tricky, risky, nonchalant,
> Anything under the sun to outwit the prosy,
> Over the tree and the long sweet cadence down,
> Over his head, make him scramble to pick up the
>   meaning,
> And now, like a posy, a pretty one plump in his hands.

Like his two young ballplayers whose only authority is the spirit of their play, Robert Francis was "uncoached" as he worked toward his new verse. His determination to devote himself fully to poetry led him to put aside even the precepts he had learned long before from his mentor Robert Frost. So in the course of his new work—beginning with *The Orb Weaver* and continuing through his next two books and his last, uncollected poems— Francis diverges more and more noticeably from his earlier "relaxed traditional" style. There is, for one thing, a different attitude toward the reader. Whereas the earlier verse was often gentle with the reader, inviting him into a poem and guiding him through it, the later poetry increasingly leaves the reader to find his own way. As he does so, he must contend with a range of address. Sometimes the narrator of a late poem speaks to a character, as in "Time and the Sergeant":

> . . . How is that anal-oriented humor now?
> Fresh and exuberant
> As ever?

Or has Old Bastard Time touched
Even you, Sergeant,
Even you?

In other poems, the narrator speaks as a character. Here
is "Siege," where menacing trees address the reader, who is
placed inside a house:

Indian-wise
We have kept moving in
With slant leaf-eyes
At windows room by room.
Your window-light is a light gloom now.
Isn't this what you wanted? . . .

The address of other poems is ironic and layered, as in
"Comedian Body," printed below in full, which concerns the
body's comic imperfections. Phrased as a prayer for forgive-
ness, the poem seems to speak not to the God who made the
body, but to the humans who must wear it.

Forgive comedian body
For featuring the bawdy.

For instance, the poor fanny
So basic and so funny.

Forgive the penis pun
That perfect two-in-one.

Forgive the blowing nose.
Forgive the ten clown toes.

And all the Noah's zoo
Of two by two by two.

Forgive the joke where
All love and art begin.

Forgive the incarnate word
Divine, obscene, absurd.

Or does Robert Francis (who began as a Christian, then lost
his faith) speak to himself in this poem about the comedy of
his own condition as a mortal and a writer, unsure of how a
higher authority might be addressed?

In addition to the unpredictability and richness of the
speaking voice, the later poetry features what Francis referred
to as the "fragmented surface." The more he wrote in his late
period, the more he tended to erase convenient transitions
between a poem's thoughts. In "The Righteous," a satiric verse
about church-goers who support the Vietnam War, the tech-
nique leads to stark juxtapositions. Here is the poem:

After the saturation bombing divine
worship after the fragmentation shells
the organ prelude the robed choir after
defoliation Easter morning the white
gloves the white lilies after the napalm
Father Son and Holy Ghost Amen.

Francis also challenged his reader with new versification
in the later poetry. A favorite technique, original with him,
he called "word-count." In *The Trouble with Francis* he de-
scribes word-count as "a way of controlling the length of a
line of poetry, not by the number of syllables it contains,
and not by the number of clusters of syllables called feet,
but by the number of whole words." "Museum Vase" offers
an example, its three-word lines matched by the three lines
of each stanza. The poem also shows Francis' developing
interest in the interplay between the printed poem and its
surrounding space.

It contains nothing.
We ask it
To contain nothing.

Having transcended use
It is endlessly
Content to be.

Still it broods
On old burdens—
Wheat, oil, wine.

In the later poems word play, an occasional device in earlier work, becomes dominant. "Comedian Body" gives one illustration; another, which contains nearly all the types of word play David Young has attributed to Francis—"doubling, rhyming, compounding, punning and echoing"—is the tiny poem "City."

In the scare
city
no scarcity
of fear
of fire
no scarcity
of goons
of guns
in the scare
city
the scar
city

By the time he wrote "Poppycock," one of his last poems, Francis was ready to declare his allegiance to lively and colorful words all by themselves:

. . . There are other cocks
to be sure.
Petcocks
weathercocks

barnyard cocks
bedroom cocks

cocksure
or cockunsure.

But to get back to poppycock
what a word!
God, what a word!
Just the word!

Keep your damn poems
only give me the words
they are made of.
Poppycock!

One way of measuring how different this later verse is from Francis' earlier work is to read his essay titled "Frost Today." Published in 1972 after Francis had made his approach to a totally original body of work, the essay not only expresses gratitude for the help the then deceased poet once gave him, but also reassesses some of the Frostian notions of poetry he once took for granted, including Frost's simple idea of literary realism. According to Frost in his famous statement about the potato, there were just two kinds of realist: the one that prefers the potato with the dirt still on it, the other that prefers his potato scrubbed clean. For Francis, whose idea about the realities possible in a poem had been stretched by his late work (and whose notion of the potato came from growing and preparing it in his own garden), the thought of choosing one acceptable realism out of the two alternatives seemed limited.

But Robert, doesn't it all depend on what you're going to do with your potato? If you're going to plant it, you'd never think of scrubbing it first. Instead of doing the potato any good, scrubbing would only do it harm by breaking the sprouts. But if you're going to boil that potato, you or anyone else would scrub it as a matter of course. If you're going to bake it and eat the skin with the rest of the potato, you'd probably do more than merely scrub it.

Having tried a variety of unrhymed and unmetered verse in his late career, including poems using his original technique of "word-count," Francis was now also ready to question Frost's well- known declaration that writing free verse was like playing tennis with the net down.

> Robert, there are other games than tennis that can be played on a tennis court, games in which a net would be irrelevant and even a hindrance, yet games fully as exacting as tennis. Further, on a tennis court dancers could dance and for them a net would be only in the way.

For in writing his way toward his truest self in poetry, Robert Francis also had to write his way beyond his mentor, Robert Frost. Francis' revolt against Frost is one of the most interesting aspects of a career whose gradual and sure development Francis related to the molting of the praying mantis. In his preface to the *Collected Poems*, speaking of himself in the third person, Francis wrote:

> As he grew older, book by book, he grew bolder and livelier. . . . It may amuse you to follow his constant comings out of himself, like the mantis in his successive moltings. . . .

The symbol of the mantis' conversion also appears in the poem "Emergence," from his next-to-last collection *Come Out into the Sun*. What reader of this poem who is familiar with the career and verse of Robert Francis will not think of the poet's own patient transformation in the slow day that led to his triumph?

> If you have watched a molting mantis
> With exquisite precision and no less
> Exquisite patience, extricate itself
> Leaf-green and like a green leaf clinging
> Little by little, leg by leg,

Out of its chitin shell, you likewise know
How one day coaxes itself out of another
Slowly, slowly by imperceptable degrees
Of gray, and having fully emerged, pauses
To dry its wings.

Robert Frost and Dramatic Speech

In a famous poem Walt Whitman called for a nation of po-
ets—of "orators, singers, musicians"—to justify him. How
pleased he would be to know today, a little over a century
later, the country's poets number in the thousands. He would
be less pleased that the great increase in America's singers
has not brought a corresponding diversity of song. There are
poets whose music and syntax are singular and arresting; in
the older generation, Adrienne Rich, Robert Creeley, and
Hayden Carruth come to mind, together with such younger
poets as Gray Jacobik and Carl Phillips. But anyone reading
contemporary verse will soon discover that the voice and gram-
mar of our poetry are often dull. The standard tone is a com-
bination of the earnest and the wistful in a standard poem
that never quite raises its voice. The cadence of that poem is
sing-song, served by sentences whose energy dissipates line
by line as it drifts to a stop. And so that annoying way of read-
ing verse common for the past fifteen years or more among
American poets at the lectern—the poet starting each sen-
tence with a certain force, and concluding it with what sound
like long notes, modulating slowly upward.

If its makers were more conscious of their audience, the
speech of today's verse would be livelier. But poets appear to
converse more with themselves than with the reader. Usually
dealing with a memory or a personal experience, they relate
their subject in such detail that the reader feels talked at rather
than to—as if he were not a participant but a convenient post.

Sometimes the reader seems not to be addressed at all.
In the opening pages of the recent anthology *New American
Poems of the 90's,* poems are directed to a variety of "you"s: a

husband; some people named in titles or epigraphs; Raoul, about a dream the poet dreamed about Raoul; and a self inside the poet's self. Discovering that he is not the principal object of the poet's address and, moreover, that the poem's you is often a device for more internalizing, the reader comes to identify himself with a narrator in one of the anthology's poems who declares, " I am tired of the tundra of the mind,/ where a few shabby thoughts hunker/ around a shabby fire." Unfortunately that narrator goes on to further thoughts about herself, addressing all the while a you named Pierre.

I am not questioning the value of poems about the self. After all, many of our best American poems, in spite of the examples I've just cited, have been written about the self, from Whitman to the present. Nor will I deal with the compelling mystery of why the tone of today's American poetry is so narrow, conveying an atmosphere of melancholy or hurt whose cause is never fully revealed. I write about the fact that too many of our poems sound the same. I suggest that, by taking more care with their syntax and directing poems to their readers, our poets might bring a new variety to their speech and their music.

For a model they could hardly do better than Robert Frost, whose stated aim was to "make poems sound as different as possible from each other," and who believed that poets should incorporate drama in their work, turning their verse outward to their audience. "Everything written," he says in his preface to *The Way Out* "is as good as dramatic"; and then he applies his thesis to the lyric, today's poem of choice. The lyric should be, he says, "sung or spoken by a person . . . in character," so it can "make itself heard." Frost goes on to explain that:

> A dramatic necessity goes deep into the nature of the sentence. Sentences are not different enough to hold attention unless they are dramatic. . . . All that can save them is the speaking

tone of voice somehow entangled in the words
and fastened tothe page for the ear of the imagi-
nation. That is all that can save poetry from sing-
song.

How various the speaking tone can be is shown in one
of Robert Frost's best-known poems, "Mending Wall." The
poem's voice, belonging to a narrator who is in character,
and for that matter in place, is open and relaxed, yet inward
and musing; it welcomes the reader, at the same time entic-
ing him into a riddle which becomes essential to the poem's
meaning.

> Something there is that doesn't love a wall,
> That sends the frozen ground-swell under it
> And spills the upper boulders in the sun.

Eventually the narrator's speculation about what might
not love a wall turns to a description of the difficulty of wall-
mending, and a questioning of the habit that has led them to
carry out the task. His range of tone as he does so moves
from seriousness to whimsy to bemusement to cajolery. As is
usual in Frost, that movement is heightened by a tension be-
tween spoken English and formal meter:

> We keep the wall between us as we go.
> To each the boulders that have fallen to each.
> And some are loaves and some so nearly balls
> We have to use a spell to make them balance:
> 'Stay where you are until our backs are turned!'
> We wear our fingers rough with handling them.
> Oh, just another kind of outdoor game,
> One on a side. It comes to little more:
> There where it is we do not need the wall:
> He is all pine and I am apple orchard.
> My apple trees will never get across
> And eat the cones under his pines, I tell him.

Where Frost got the dramatic speech of his poetry is worth recalling. It did not come from listening to himself talk, but from listening to other people in the place where he lived. In an early interview he explained that he discovered poetic speech by copying into a poem "the character of a man" who often spoke to him at his farm in Derry; afterward, he told his interviewer, he conducted a study of the possible uses of "human speech" for his poems so they would have what he called a "psychology of sound." In a still earlier letter Frost declared that the true cadences of poetry could only be derived "fresh from talk" of others, and then he proceeded to give examples of poems that were guided by that notion. What he ended up with was poetic speech that resembled American talk with a New England accent. If readers are engaged by Frost's speaking voice, it is not only the tonal variation they are drawn to, then; they are also drawn to the idiom, which is by design not far from their own.

So important is the reader as audience for Frost's dramatic sentence that his typical poem is made to be *said* by the reader, who must himself furnish its tones of voice, participating in the creation of meaning as he does so. "For Once, Then, Something" and "The Road Not Taken" demonstrate the process and the special access it provides. In the former poem a man who stares into wells suddenly sees through his own reflection on the water's surface to find a mysterious something that could be, as he tells us, "Truth" or merely "a pebble of quartz." The poem ends with the phrase "For once, then, something." Depending how the reader *says* the sentence, it could express the narrator's sense of triumph for what he has been able to perceive, or the narrator's awareness of the limits of his perception. In a like way the last lines of "The Road Not Taken"—"I took the one less traveled by,/ and that has made all the difference"—might suggest that the speaker is congratulating himself for having chosen the right life-road when he was a young man, or, contrarily, that he is mocking himself for having assumed in his youth that his choice was the right one. In both poems the ultimate meaning depends on how the reader reads, and in what tone. Both poems are so open to his participation that neither is finished until the reader (Frost would enjoy the pun) says so.

As I've already implied, the psychology of sound which the audience brings to life is not all there is to Robert Frost's music. So when one reads his poetry with the ear (which is, Frost once said, the only true writer or reader) one discovers the interplay of meter and voice, of what he called sound and "the sound of sense." Returning to the terms of drama, he wrote in his essay, "The Figure a Poem Makes" that the "possibilities for music from the dramatic tones of meaning struck across the rigidity of meter are endless," and he illustrated the point with poems like "Birches," whose opening image of birch trees bent across the straighter trees of the woods seems to illustrate the interplay of crooked and straight in the way the poem is said:

> When I see birches bend to left and right
> Across the lines of straighter, darker trees,
> I like to think some boy's been swinging them.

The more one becomes aware of the importance of meter in the figure a Frost poem makes, the better one understands his assertion that "For my pleasure I would as soon write free verse as play tennis with the net down."

Yet Frost left contemporaries who write free verse a good deal to learn about poetic form despite that much-quoted statement. The source of the instruction is the *shape* of his sentence, an essential part of a poem's drama. It is sentence-shape he has in mind when he says that the poem should "tell how it can"—and when he declares that the poem's figure "runs a course of lucky events," unfolding "by surprise" as it goes, riding like "a piece of ice on a hot stove . . . on its own melting."

How he makes the sentence move in this restless way, unpredictably and yet smoothly, is in part by a technique familiar to practitioners of free verse: the interplay of the sentence and the line. In his longer poems especially Frost enjambs his lines at least as much as he end-stops them, releasing the sentence to its own active life. So, while the movement of the sentence may parallel that of the line, it often runs a contrary way, continuing beyond one line and then another, perhaps coming to a rest at a caesura. What drives Frost's lively sentence, barely within the control of the line, is a particular syntax. Sometimes his sentence opens with a dependent clause or phrase that is aimed toward the verb of the independent clause which follows. Sometimes it begins with a statement that becomes conditional as it travels, by way of conjunctions, to later statements. Almost always the total effect is of action to be revealed or completed just beyond this line, and then the next, until we find ourselves at the end of the poem. There, a certain tone of voice may cause the sentence to linger, even though it has come to a close.

We have already seen how such a conclusion works in "The Road Not Taken." This poem also illustrates how the Frostian sentence runs its course of lucky events from line to line, through all the twists and turns of end-stop and enjambment, clause and conjunction, to the not-so-final stop of the last period.

> Two roads diverged in a yellow wood,
> And sorry I could not travel both
> And be one traveler, long I stood
> And looked down one as far as I could
> To where it bent in the undergrowth;
>
> Then took the other, as just as fair,
> And having perhaps the better claim,
> Because it was grassy and wanted wear
> Though as for that, the passing there
> Had worn them really about the same,
>
> And both that morning equally lay
> In leaves no step had trodden black.
> Oh, I kept the first for another day!

Yet knowing how way leads on to way,
I doubted if I would ever come back.

I shall be telling this with a sigh
Somewhere ages and ages hence:
Two roads diverged in a wood, and I—
I took the one less traveled by,
And that has made all the difference.

In its grammar alone, it is a masterly performance. How much Frost's syntax contributes to the interplay of line and sentence is quickly seen when one measures it against the dull syntax of so much of today's verse. In work by contemporary poets the typical sentence—the sing-song sentence of the wistful tone referred to at the outset of this essay—is often nearly static. It opens with a declaration, which is often followed by qualifiers, like the participial phrases of Robin Behn's "Late Search":

> . . . I knew you only
> by the glint of water, reflected
> off some deeper, moving thing like clean
> white bones, or fish.
> Vermont, late fall, the sun
> backing off a bit each day—it seemed a good
> place to find you, heading north
> into the dark.
>   I found an inn
> by the river and lay all night, the wheels
> still in my head and the river
> and the river road stretching on like
> your breath in my body . . .

Occasionally the opening statement is followed by qualifiers of another sort—appositives, say, like those in Timothy Liu's "Passion." The colon that introduces the appositives of Liu's poem is standard equipment in sentences of this kind.

By mid-afternoon, all is imprecision:
the brittle poppies in the garden
a bright suffusion of crimson and saffron
the honey bees darting
in and out of the miniature roses
beyond the topiary, two children
in a maze of bronze trees reaching out
to support the sky . . .

In other poems the opening statement leads to a series of direct objects—or to objects of the preposition, sampled here in "Conversation in Woodside," by Kim Addonizio:

I thought of all the evidence
against us, against the pink poppies

opening in a glass vase, the fragrant candles,
the living room where the others were dancing
while we kept on, talking about loss . . .

It may also lead to objects of the infinitive, like the clauses in Mark Cox's "Geese":

But I wanted so badly . . .
to forget how, driving home, I was fooled
by half an acre of decoys
and some camouflage netting,

how I wanted to honk but didn't,
and how the whole scene made me realize
that mannequins mate for life too,
in department stores . . .

In "The Oasis Motel," William Olsen links his initial declaration to a succession of predicate nouns in clause form, another procedure typical of today's verse:

I touch you like the waves admire the weirs.
It is themselves they push out from, toward what

they are a part of, and it is transportation,
and this is why palms rustle, why the moon
drops shamelessly below the horizontal
off the Gulf of Mexico, and why you, too,

are something else, utterly familiar.

This passage from "Autumnal," by Lynn McMahon, fol-
lows the initial statement with predicate nouns, too, going
on to a clause, three objects of the infinitive, and another
clause.

> . . . But what
> I felt was the pavement pressing up through my
> Pea coat and scarf, the cold recalling me to the
> ordinary
>
> Where I was enjoined to release the ring, the film,
> The astronomy of meanings whose secrets I was
> Allowed to enter, for a moment, and immediately
> Forget . . .

Yet, however complex the sentence may become, and
however the poet may try—as Deborah Digges tries in this
next excerpt from "Secrets"—to enliven those complexities
by pauses and enjambments that carry the eye across stanzas,
the effect is of a thought process winding down rather than
winding up, of a sentence dying with a dying fall:

> Some nights, a thousand miles inland, a storm
> blowing across the frozen fields,
>
> I'd fall asleep pretending I heard the ocean,
> heard the earth's ancient machinery's
> creak and roar, the first myths gathering in the air
>
> above the water like flocks pulled star
> to star, prophesying,
> in their spirals, hands gesturing towards language,

the neurons sparking as the animal
face contorts,
as the eyes burn into the eyes of the listener

and the lips spit, struggle
to form an O.

But wait, one might argue, doesn't the content of such poems justify the grammar and tone of the entropic sentence? I can only reply that, if it does, the repetition of the sentence suggests that in ways not immediately apparent, content itself must be redundant. This much is certain: in their grammar contemporary poets have turned the Robert Frost sentence upside-down, substituting their opening declaration for his syntax of delay. The effects of the two approaches could not be more different. Whereas in Frost the sentence is unpredictable, unfolding in its action, the sentence of today's poetry is predictable, unfolding only in the interpretations the writer adds to an action already completed. Whereas the Frost sentence is spontaneous and wild (to use one of his favorite terms for a poem), the contemporary sentence is self-conscious and programmatic. It is obvious which of the two grammars better addresses a time in human history that is itself unpredictable, demanding intellectual improvisation.

It is also obvious which one is less dramatic. Writing enthusiastically about the poetry of his fellow New Englander, Edwin Arlington Robinson, Frost said, "Robinson could make lyric talk like drama." Let today's poets seek similar praise for their own work, listening less to each other than to language as it is spoken around them. Let them address their readers in character with dramatic speech and instill life into their poetry.

IV.
Places in the Dark

Dark Dreams, Dark Sayings

In part 4 of his well-known poem "The Hill Wife," Robert Frost describes a traumatic event in the life of his central figure, a newly married woman who lives in the isolation of a hill farm. Lying in bed night after night as her husband sleeps, the hill wife watches a "dark pine" outside her window "trying the window latch" of her bedroom. Small as the event is, its recurrence brings repeated and worrisome associations to mind. In a trance-like state before she falls asleep, she imagines that the pine's boughs are "hands," and "a little bird/ Before the mystery of glass." Eventually, the tree threatens her in a recurring nightmare, and at the end of Frost's sequence when the hill wife, who seems oddly charmed by fern and black alder at the edge of the clearing, disappears, it is as though the trees have spirited her away.

The story of the hill wife suggests the steps by which psychological trauma often happens: first comes the event that caused the trauma; then, in a response related to dreaming, the traumatized person replays the event, sometimes having actual dreams about it. In the end the trauma may so trouble the daydreamer and night-dreamer that he or she is taken over by it.

What went wrong for the hill wife, the psychotherapist might say, is that she never found a way to talk about her problems. Perhaps this is what Frost himself wants to convey in his poem's opening, where he tells us that "she had no saying dark enough/ For the dark pine." But I like to think that Frost had the sayings of poetry in mind when he wrote those lines. He was, after all, a poet who often included darkness in his work, and who at the end of his life reportedly kept a light on in his bedroom while he slept, afraid to turn it off. Though the hill wife cannot find the saying that will break the menacing spell of her darkness, it is not hard to imagine that Robert Frost, by using his poem to explore her situation, could for the moment free himself from whatever darkness may have troubled him, allowing her to enter the woods he did not wish (in this poem and many others where he remains outside a wooded interior) to enter himself.

Of course Frost could not have had his say about the hill wife without the creative process of conjuring her up, which is itself a sort of dreaming, though a more complex sort than the recurrent dreaming associated with the trauma. The poet's dreaming, after all, results in language. Moreover, it brings insight to the things dreamed, as the compulsive replaying of a traumatic event cannot do. The difference between the two kinds of dreaming was brought home to me when I worked on a poem about a traumatic experience with my stepfather's violence I had as a teenager. I forgot about the experience not long after it happened, but when my stepfather died, it rose up again in my memory, and I went over it again and again, evidencing each time, no doubt, the inward stare common to daydreamers—or, in the case of the traumatized, daymarers. One morning at my notebook, having worn the event down to essentials, I started this poem:

AFTER MY STEPFATHER'S DEATH

> Again it is the moment before I left home
> for good, and my mother is sitting quietly
> in the front seat while my stepfather pulls me
> and my suitcase out of the car and begins
> hurling my clothes, though now
> I notice for the first time how the wind
> unfolds my white shirt and puts its slow
> arm in the sleeve of my blue shirt and lifts them
> all into the air above our heads so beautifully
> I want to shout and him to stop and look up
> at what he has made, but of course when I turn

to him, a small man, bitter even this young
that the world will not go his way, my stepfather
still moves in his terrible anger, closing the trunk,
and closing himself into the car as hard as he can,
and speeding away into the last years of his life.

No poem is easy to write, but his one was more difficult
than most. The big problem was separating the traumatic
event I had dreamed from the poem I needed to write about
it. In the event, the clothes my angry stepfather threw fell
into the roadside ditch and onto hay stubble in the nearby
field. I spent days describing the clothes on the ground as I
remembered them, but no description seemed to take the
poem where it had to go. Putting my poem aside in frustra-
tion, I returned to it a while later and dreamed the story dif-
ferently, seeing the clothes opening into the air. Suddenly
they became a means of revealing my stepfather's inner life.
Without even mentioning the soap carvings from his child-
hood I had once found in the house or the drawing from his
adolescence that hung in the living room, I was able to speak
about the unrealized capacity to create beautiful things I
sensed in him, and in that way to intensify our missed con-
nection during his life. Altering the trauma by redreaming it,
I went deeper into my relationship with my stepfather than I
had ever been, turning what had been a story of pain and
fear into a kind of love story. To put it another way, I found a
saying dark enough, and full enough, for the experience I
once had and as a result, I was able to dispel some of the
trauma's darkness.

While I redreamed the trauma of "After My Stepfather's
Death," in another poem, "The Abandonment," I dreamed
the details of a traumatic event I never witnessed. The poem
describes the heart attack that took my younger brother's life
when he was forty-three years old—a heart attack that fol-
lowed six months of daily running. Eventually I would write a
long poem called "My Brother Running," attempting to dis-
cover what he was running to, and running from. But before

I could begin that poem, I had to complete this one which, as it turned out, opened the way to the long poem.

What drew me to "The Abandonment" was not only the terrible news of my brother's death, but the impotence I felt in the face of it. All I had to go on in making my poem about his heart attack were the few facts I had learned from an early morning phone call and the talk at his funeral—these and so much pain that when I sat down to write, what I wanted to utter was a long scream. The poem I ended up with was in one long, ragged sentence:

THE ABANDONMENT

Climbing on top of him and breathing
into his mouth this way she could be showing her
desire except that when she draws back
from him to make her little cries
she is turning to her young son just
coming into the room to find his father my
    brother
on the bed with his eyes closed and the slightest
smile on his lips as if when they
both beat on his chest as they do now
he will come back from the dream he is enjoying
so much he cannot hear her calling his name
louder and louder and the son saying get up
get up discovering both of them discovering
for the first time that all along
he has lived in this body this thing
with shut lids dangling its arms
that have nothing to do with him and everything
they can ever know the wife listening weeping
at his chest and the mute son who will never
forget how she takes the face into her hands now
as if there were nothing in the world
but the face and breathes oh
breathes into the mouth which does not
    breathe back.

How can a poet, by dreaming deeply into the thing which most troubles him, restore himself? Even knowing from my own writing the power that comes from naming the darkness, I am still amazed by the process. Nevertheless, by using that long sentence to describe my brother's limp body and the attempt by his wife and son to bring him back to life, I was beginning to extricate myself from the news that replayed in my mind. I have already referred to the distinguishing feature of insight in the dreaming of a poem, and as I look back on "The Abandonment," I see how important the insight it offered was to my healing. For the poem helped me to discover a compassion for two actual witnesses who had been devastated by the heart attack, and thus feel sorrows other than my own. It also led me to an image I returned to in "My Brother Running"—the image, that is, of my brother's smile, which seems to imply he is conscious in some eyes-closed world his wife cannot reach by calling his name and the poem itself cannot reach either, for all of its naming. Whether the smile is really a sign of my brother's presence in this other world, or a deceptive last reflex of the face is an unanswered question in the poem, but by imagining that smile and the conspiratorial intimacy it carried for me in life, I found a grim sort of comfort and hope.

In both of the poems I have discussed so far, I began with the bad dream of the trauma, reshaping it into the good, restorative dream of the poem. But in "A Dream of Herman" I put the bad dream aside entirely, replacing it with the poem's good dream. Like the other verses, "A Dream of Herman" was written in response to the death of a family member—my father-in-law Herman, who died in the hospital after a long illness, leaving my wife inconsolable. I didn't need to be told all the details of my wife's bad dreams, waking and sleeping, that followed the event; I had my own troubling dreams. To counter them, I imagined that I had dreamt of a car ride, narrating the poem to suggest I was sharing the dream and its happiness with Diane.

A DREAM OF HERMAN

I was driving the old Dodge wagon
again, with Coke cans rolling
to the front at stop signs,
and you rubbing the dash
every so often to thank the car
for not needing the spare tire
we hadn't fixed. We were on a trip
that felt like going to your father's camp, only
we never got there and didn't care.
It was a beautiful day, just enough wind
coming into the back to make the kids
squint with pure pleasure
as it scribbled their hair, and your mother
patted them, saying what a nice ride it was
in the odd, small voice
she used only for your father.
It was then in the rearview mirror I saw him,
wearing the same brown cardigan he always wore
and putting on the shining bell
of his saxophone as if just back
from an intermission. You were smiling,
and suddenly I saw the reason
we were traveling together
and did not want to stop
was Herman, who just sat there
in the cargo space, breathing the scale
until the whole family sat back
in their seats, and then he lifted his sax
and opened one more song as wide
and delicate as the floating trees.

As the poem suggests, Herman was a musician, a
bandleader who played the saxophone with considerable skill
well into his sixties. Yet for all his gifts as a performer, he was
a shy and quiet man—the very sort of mortal who might sud-
denly appear in the cargo space to breathe the scale, delight-
ing my wife and family once again.

"A Dream of Herman" did not lift the trauma entirely away, any more than the other poems I've cited did; the loss of loved one leaves a mark that never quite disappears. In the end, the poem helped me more than Diane, the person for whom I thought I was writing it. In a little way, though, I think it helped Diane too—not only because it showed Herman was still with us, but because it paid a special tribute to family love. In its light and affirmation "A Dream of Herman" is different from the other two poems I have quoted. However, all three deal with fear and sorrow and death, and in each one compassion is paramount, making possible the poem's freeing insight, just as Robert Frost's compassion for the hill wife made the insight of his poem sequence possible. In their different ways, then, these poems about trauma are also love poems, suggesting that when trauma comes, there may be sayings sufficiently dark, and light, to repel it.

Places in the Dark

In his book *The Return of the Vanishing American* Leslie Fiedler remarks that geography in the United States is mythical and that American writers, responding to this geography, have written books that divide the country up into four mythical regions. What results, he says, are not only Westerns, but Easterns, Southerns, and Northerns. Never mind that Fiedler's definition of the Northern (set in a "hostile environment . . . the weather deep winter") tends to stereotype New England literature. The term Northern sticks, as does his comment that it "works better in verse than in prose." For the Northern as I know it is a genre that explores interior and psychic spaces, as poetry does best. New Englanders, after all, have a long habit of inwardness, forced by an onerous climate to stay indoors through much of the year, and living in a wooded landscape whose geography hides itself, making even a trip to the next town by car feel like a journey into the interior. Little wonder that those early white settlers, the Puritans, found an environment exactly suited to searching for evidence of wickedness or spiritual improvement in the tricky depths of their own hearts. Their compressed personal narratives in poetry and prose concentrating on the drama of the inner life are the origin of the Northern.

Some of the most characteristic and moving New England poems I know—that is to say, Northerns—are set not in the winter but at night. Given the frequency of short days and long nights on the New England calendar, it should surprise no one that nighttime darkness appears often in New England verse, even in the poetic prose of the Transcendentalists. When we typecast Emerson and Thoreau as Romantics who are inspired only by the light of a daytime nature, we forget Thoreau's chapter on solitude in *Walden*, which opens with a tribute to the darkness of evening, or entries in Emerson's journal such as the one dated May 11, 1838, where he tells the reader to "Come out of your warm, angular house, resounding with few voices, into the chill, grand, instantaneous night, with such a Presence as a full moon in the clouds, and you are struck with poetic wonder." Emerson continues:

> In the instant you leave far behind all human relations, wife mother and child, and live only with the savages—water, air, light, carbon, lime, and granite. I think of Kuhleborn. I become a moist, cold element . . . Frogs pipe; waters far off tinkle; dry leaves hiss; grass bends and rustles, and I have died out of the human world and come to feel a strange . . . sympathy and existence.

With this passage we return to the theme of inwardness, since his darkness is linked with developing a new sense of self. As it happens, Emerson's description of night is close to the New England poem I have in mind. That poem, too, portrays a darkness set apart from the warmth and security of social relations, a darkness that offers the isolato who enters it an altered awareness.

A case in point is Emily Dickinson's "We Grow Accustomed to the Dark." We are introduced to the night of the poem in its first two stanzas, where the central action is established: a figure is led in darkness to a road by a neighbor, who then departs with her lamp, leaving the figure, a stand-in for the collective "we" of the poem, to find the way without illumination—or, as Dickinson puts it, to "fit our Vision to the Dark." The poem's action becomes complicated when, in stanza three, she links the night with the psychological darkness of depression or despair:

And so of larger—Darknesses—
Those Evenings of the Brain—
When not a Moon disclose a sign—
Or Star—come out—within—

With no moon or star to light the way, Dickinson's night is a good deal more forbidding than Emerson's. In the rest of her poem she shows how hazardous the travel there is for those brave enough to attempt it.

The Bravest—grope a little—
And sometimes hit a Tree
Directly on the Forehead—
But as they learn to see—

Either the Darkness alters—
Or something in the sight
Adjusts itself to Midnight—
And Life steps almost straight.

Yet this is not, Dickinson implies, a hopeless dark, since as we take our faltering steps and missteps, we may learn to see and, however imperfectly, walk, either because of some resource in the eye or the dark's own alteration. The possible result of such brave walking, that is, facing our inner darknesses and carrying on in spite of them, is that we may take the steps of our journey as whole selves, not only with our feet, but in a fuller way, with our lives.

The night Dickinson features in "We Grow Accustomed to the Dark," bleaker and more difficult to navigate than Emerson's, provides a key to the other poems I am considering in this essay, as does her emphasis on the interior world, whose darknesses, she tells us, are even "larger" than the night dark itself. Consider Edwin Arlington Robinson's "Mr. Flood's Party," in which another night walker, Eben Flood, tries to make his way. Having refilled his liquor jug in town, Flood climbs alone toward his "forsaken upland hermitage," a sad old man caught in time and social change, without friends and neighbors. Bravery may have served the walker of Dickinson's poem; in the darkness Robinson presents, bravery will do no good. There seems nothing left for Flood, sipping alcohol "amid the silver loneliness" of moonlight, but to turn inward and invent his own company—a festive alter ego who receives him warmly and encourages further drinking:

> "Well, Mr. Flood, we have not met like this
> In a long time, and many a change has come
> To both of us, I fear, since last it was
> We had a drop together. Welcome home!"

Through his fantasy of a double, Robinson's character manages temporary relief from problems too great for him to solve. Eben Flood's inward-seeking is different from that of Puritan autobiography, and the strange sympathy and existence he finds on his walk scarcely resembles the kind advocated by Emerson in his journal. In its broad outlines, nonetheless, Robinson's poem is a nighttime Northern, separating Flood from the warmth of human relations, and testing such inner resources as he has.

The bleak darkness of Dickinson and Robinson that forces night walkers to consider ultimate things appears also in Jane Kenyon's "Let Evening Come."

> Let the light of late afternoon
> shine through chinks in the barn, moving
> up the bales as the sun moves down.
>
> Let the cricket take up chafing
> as a woman takes up her needles
> and her yarn. Let evening come.
>
> Let the dew collect on the hoe abandoned
> in long grass. Let the stars appear
> and the moon disclose her silver horn.

Let the fox go back to its sandy den.
Let the wind die down. Let the shed
go black inside. Let evening come.

To the bottle in the ditch, to the scoop
in the oats, to air in the lung
let evening come.

Let it come, as it will, and don't
be afraid. God does not leave us
comfortless, so let evening come.

Those who interpret "Let Evening Come" solely as a re-
ligious consolation for all who struggle with mortality and
death are missing the poem's true dimension. In the first
place, Jane Kenyon was relentlessly autobiographical in her
verse, religious or otherwise, creating poem by poem a provi-
sional order for herself against the formlessness of dark
thoughts and emotional distress. In the second place Kenyon
often associated evening with sorrow and depression, just as
Emily Dickinson did in "We Grow Accustomed to the Dark."
So while "Let Evening Come" may be viewed as a public poem
in which she consoles her readers about the inevitability of
death, it is also a personal poem in which she attempts to
console herself about the emotional and psychological death
that depression brings. Finding images for the failed defense
against melancholy ("the bottle in the ditch") and the work
depression interrupts ("the scoop/ in the oats") even as she
welcomes the oncoming blackness of evening, Kenyon shows
a courage comparable to that of the character in Dickinson's
poem, her bravery inspired by religious belief.

The darkness of Hayden Carruth's "The Cows at Night"
has an allure that makes it different from the darknesses of
Kenyon, Robinson, and Dickinson. Though the moon has
set, leaving only "faint stars," the narrator tells us he likes
driving through this night, describing the experience at the
beginning of the poem in such an appealing way, we over-
look for the moment his lack of destination, his aimlessness.

Suddenly he comes upon a herd of cows, which startles him
and draws him out of the car with his flashlight:

> I stopped, and took my flashlight
> to the pasture fence. They turned
> to me where they lay, sad
>
> and beautiful faces in the dark,
> and I counted them—forty
> near and far in the pasture,
>
> turning to me, sad and beautiful
> like girls very long ago
> who were innocent, and sad
>
> because they were innocent,
> and beautiful because they were
> sad . . . .

Is it the mute and guileless acceptance by these crea-
tures of their confinement, or their unreflecting beauty as he
discovers them in the dark that compels the narrator? How-
ever one explains their impact in this strange and moving
encounter, the cows ultimately suggest to him all the inno-
cence and sorrow of the creatural life. When he turns his
flashlight off, he becomes aware of the night in a way that is
different from his initial descriptions of it: it is now "that great
darkness." Standing alone in it, and feeling perhaps how lost
the beautiful and innocent cows are in such a dark, he feels
the impulse to stay with them; yet he realizes he can do noth-
ing about their predicament, since all creatures everywhere
are lost in the darkness—including himself in this moment, a
man without reasons or answers:

> . . . for how
>
> in that great darkness could I explain
> anything, anything at all.

Up against the ultimates and lacking the inner resources to deal with his night, Carruth's narrator is less fortunate than the speakers and characters of the other poems, but for one thing: the darkness or nature itself seems to respond to him. At the end of the verse, as the narrator stands by the fence in turmoil and anguish, Carruth tells us that "very gently it began to rain." These words are the more significant because they appear in one final line that departs from the poem's established form of three-line stanzas. Has he misunderstood the meaning of the night that surrounds him and the cows? Could the deep compassion he feels for all creatures have elicited the night's blessing? Like Emily Dickinson in "We Grow Accustomed to the Dark," the narrator here may well wonder whether in this moment "the darkness alters"—and why.

No poet seems a more obvious fit for the tradition of the nighttime Northern I have been tracing than Robert Frost. In Frost's poems the deeper darkness is somewhere beyond the clearing—a threatening place toward which his characters travel again and again. Yet the fit is not so convenient as it first appears because Frost's Northern is often incomplete. Contrary to the figures of poems by Dickinson, Robinson, Kenyon, and Carruth, his characters either refuse to enter their darkness, or they claim to have visited the dark while screening the actual experience from us. So the speaker in "Stopping by Woods on a Snowy Evening," lingering with his horse outside the woods which he finds "lovely, dark and deep" decides that he must return to the world of social obligations, the very world from which Emerson advocated a retreat. And the narrator of "Acquainted with the Night" declares that he has journeyed into the dark beyond his town without ever taking us there. The reluctance of Frost's narrators to risk a lack of control and delve into the deeper darkness reminds us of what the poems by other poets being considered here ultimately offer. For as the narrators and characters of these poems surrender themselves to the night world, come what may, they provide a view of the darkness and their capacity to deal with it that would be impossible otherwise. Moreover, they are often led—as in "We Grow Accustomed to the Dark," "Let Evening Come," and "The Cows at Night"—to uncommon insights, as we are, journeying with them.

Clearly the authors of these figures have benefited as well. Their verses about the dark world, including several not cited in this essay, are among the most moving and profound poems they have written. How has Robert Frost's unwillingness to explore the dark beyond the clearing affected his poetry? The question is worth asking, particularly since in one of his night poems he touches on the issue himself. Consider "Come In."

> As I came to the edge of the woods,
> Thrush music—hark!
> Now if it was dusk outside,
> Inside it was dark.
>
> Too dark in the woods for a bird
> By slight of wing
> To better its perch for the night,
> Though it could still sing.
>
> The last of the light of the sun
> That had died in the west
> Still lived for one song more
> In a thrush's breast.
>
> Far in the pillared dark
> Thrush music went—
> Almost like a call to come in
> To the dark and lament.
>
> But no, I was out for stars:
> I would not come in.
> I meant not even if asked,
> And I hadn't been.

The poem features that familiar Frostian predicament of a speaker at the edge of the woods who feels the attraction of darkness. This time, though, Frost's narrator is enticed by thrush, whose music, as in Hardy, suggests the song of poetic art. The trouble is that he cannot go to the thrush without traveling "far in the pillared dark" and opening himself to sorrow—an essential element of the nighttime Northern. Refusing to leave the clearing, the speaker ends the poem by rationalizing: the thrush's music might not have been an invitation after all, and even if it were, it wasn't an invitation for him. He is "out for stars," he tells us; yet, for all of his bravado, we can't avoid the conclusion that he has chosen a safer sort of aspiration. Nor can we escape the impression that by guiding his speaker away from the woods, Frost has forsaken an encounter crucial to his poetry. Grateful for the vision of those New England poets who dared to venture into the dark, we may also speculate how much greater Robert Frost, great as he was, might have been if in poems like this one he put aside his reservations and entered the darkness without condition.

My Finite Eyes

What they see—the nurse watching the operation and the surgeon making his incision in the center of my left eye—I try to picture: the eye clamped open and staring up from its hole in the blue drape placed on my face. Grotesque as it is, the image doesn't bother me. I am peacefully sedated, and I gaze with my other eye into a cloudy blue that is the exact color of my contentment. Far off to the left, as if I were dreaming it, I am aware of a puddle, shaking in blue light. This is all I know of what the surgeon is doing, though I detect, in the long pauses of his conversation, his absorption.

"I've got something in my eye," we sometimes say, though the thing we have is more *on* the eye than in it. A cataract, on the other hand, is in it—the lens become an opaque pebble that makes lights splay and words disappear. My cataract is what the doctor has taken out. And now, the next day, he reaches for my eye patch to see how he has done. I think of the scene from the old movie: Bogart as an escaped convict, watching the doctor peel the bandages from his facial surgery. Only the doctor knows what the convict looks like now in his new identity, yet you can tell from the doctor's smile he is pleased. I examine the face of my own surgeon, but he just frowns, swinging a chin rest, then a light toward me. There is silence as I position my chin and stare into more blue, a furry circle of it this time, and he explores with his painful point of white light. At last, I hear his word for what he has discovered: beautiful. Like Bogart himself, I am now a free man.

On the way home in a dry snowfall, my son driving, I recall Emerson, who wrote in his essay "Nature" that while he was in the woods, nothing could befall him—"no disgrace, no calamity (leaving me my eyes) which nature cannot repair." Leaving me my eyes! Enclosing the phrase in parentheses, Emerson snatched his eyes right out of that famous covenant with nature as if to say, These, I don't make deals with. Pleased by my doctor's report, and glad to live in a century when surgeons can repair the things that nature cannot, I am drawn to winter on the road as I have never quite seen it. There is a thin dust of snow across the tail lights of the car ahead that gives them a soft, bright glow. Past the town sign, gusts of snow swirl, tangle, and edge away from a hundred white cracks in the pavement as we pass. But more compelling still are the snowy woods that come toward us, opening to let the road through, then wider to let us through, the high branches of pines sheltering us for a quarter-mile.

You are too young for cataracts! a friend exclaims when I tell him about the success of my operation. In fact, I am exactly the right age. My father got them in his fifties, inheriting from his elders the early cataract gene which he then passed on to me. The day after surgery, I think of what it must have been like for my father, who left the family in my childhood, when both of his lenses went dark. Victimized by high blood pressure and an ailing heart, he was considered a poor risk for anesthesia, so his cataracts were never removed. In his last months his vision got so bad, according to a relative, he labored in the backyard garden lying on his side. That close to his work, he could just make out the difference between the seed plants and the weeds. What his thoughts were as he weeded, having left some of his own seed behind to grow as it would without his help, the relative didn't say. Only that he lived in a dimness, unable to read or to bear bright lights, until the day he died. The very age of my father as he lay in that garden, I feel the more keenly the sadness of his life, and recall, too, all the trouble he passed on to me apart from my cataracts. I am relieved I have at least been able to rid myself of this trouble.

Unfortunately, however, my relief does not last. Concerned about my double vision a week after the operation, I consult a new surgeon, filling in while my own is on vacation. The new doctor, who has nothing to do with gentleness or care, shakes drops in my eye and reaches for her tools. Then in she goes, pressing a contact lens against my eye with the narrow end of a metal cone. Holding the cone fast, she shines a light inside it that is so bright, I shut my other eye and pop the contact lens out. "I'm sorry," I tell her, hoping—I am so compliant, so willing to have her savage me this way—she'll see the error of her aggressiveness. But she is now impatient with me, and even more aggressive. When the session is finished, I am wandering in the parking lot, blind in one eye and unable to find my car. Going up and down the rows, I hear her voice in my head—its certainty that I've done something wrong. "You must be more careful in the future," it says. "That implant has become decentered."

"At fifty we're so fragile," Robert Lowell—that chronicler of eye problems—wrote about his increasing nearsightedness in "Myopia: a Night." Waiting the next four days for my vacationing surgeon to return, I feel the middle-age fragility Lowell referred to. And I remember the bad eye trouble Lowell described in another poem, "Eye and Tooth"—his cut cornea, which caused a turmoil of pain, memory, and self-recrimination. For I now begin to suffer my own self-recrimination, convincing myself in the end that the substitute doctor is right: the decentered implant is my fault. I've bent over too far or lifted something heavy without thinking and caused the nearly invisible hooks at the left and right of the implant to slip. Yet when my surgeon sees me again, he does not accuse me. The decentering could have been caused by any number of things, he says, even by a small vacuum that may have settled, unbeknownst, under the implant. He draws a Mickey Mouse eye with a slipped implant to show me how my eye looks; meanwhile, I watch the double image of his thumb and fingers moving on the tablet, wondering if his hand itself could be the culprit. No, I decide; too many others have praised this surgeon's work. The relative stillness of that drawing hand, which barely moved moments ago when I shook it, shows how steady it would be under pressure.

So I go for surgery again, wearing the blue drape on my face while my surgeon's hand makes a wider incision for a new implant—this one big enough that no subsequent slipping will matter. The day after, I return for a third rerun of myself as Bogart watching my surgeon remove the bandage. For I have already been in his office twice now with a patch, the first time two years ago, after cataract surgery on my right eye.

In the weeks following that operation, just as I had gotten used to bright sun without my special dark glasses, a catastrophe developed: my retina tore in two places, with the threat of a retinal detachment. After the new surgery on my left eye, the doctor warns me to be on the lookout for the sudden flashes of light that indicate a tearing of the retina. It is my bad luck to notice the flashes just days later. I make an immediate appointment with him. Eye surgeons mend retinal tears, I learned from my earlier experience, by applying laser beams carefully calibrated in intensity. By my side once more to apply them in his dark room, my doctor wears his odd, cone-shaped hat made of metal. "Six hundred," he says to an assistant and presses a pedal, sending white light into my eye from the point of his hat. "Seven hundred," he says. "Nine hundred." Each time, I feel a dull pain and simultaneously behold something I did not see in my first treatment: a large, beautiful planet that contains several tiny, red rivers. Listening to the numbers and watching that mysterious orb in the dark, I could be seated among the priests of an occult religion, learning by some strange ritual the secrets of the universe. Then I realize what I observe is no planet; it is a reflection of my eye.

Yet to see the eye as so vast a thing is not to misrepresent it. For in losing our eyes, we would lose nothing less than the whole world. We would be like the speaker in Emily Dickinson's poem 327, who "got [her] eye put out," and now yearns for all she once had:

. . . But were it told to me—Today—
That I might have the sky
For mine—I tell you that my Heart
Would split, for size of me—

The meadows—mine—
The Mountains—mine—
All Forests—Stintless Stars—
As much of Noon as I could take
Between my finite eyes—

The Motions of the Dipping Birds—
The Morning's Amber Road—
For mine—to look at when I liked—
The News would strike me dead—

Months after she played the sightless narrator of this poem, Dickinson suffered an eye disorder that actually took away her sight, suddenly experiencing the "death" she had earlier imagined, without forests or mountains, dipping birds or amber road. By what marvel of perception this poet was able to look ahead to her own malady and prepare herself for the treatments that finally healed her, it would be hard to say. I only know that now, with my sight intact, I have returned more than once to Dickinson's poem 327 for its tribute to sight and its suggestion about the insight of art. Finite though we human observers are, I am grateful we are allowed both kinds of vision.

V.
End Notes

Notes on Poets, Poets Teaching, and Poetry

Much has been written about the influence of the academy on the writer who teaches there. But what about the influence a writer may have on the academy? On our way to the airport after her visit at the University of Maine at Farmington, Lucille Clifton, speaking of poets who teach, asks: "Who else can teach students about the need to serve something larger than themselves?" Later, she remarks on the limits of the academy's approach to education: "It teaches one way of knowing," she says, "and it's the easiest way." Clifton adds she no longer felt ashamed of lacking an academic degree once she realized that having none, she was better able to show students other ways of knowing.

*

Could it be that creative writing has become so popular in colleges today because of our students' need to reclaim the personal and moral uses of language in a period when advertising has so corrupted it? On some level, the students in my classes feel this need, I think. Consequently, I take satisfaction from the main lesson in language they learn there: telling the truth.

*

"I don't know how to fill up all those pages," says one of my best student poets, now taking a fiction class. Time will tell whether she's too much a poet to to be shown the ways of fiction, as a few students seem to be. But it is clear that poets think differently than do fiction writers. They see what they see in a flash—a sudden insight that gathers a cluster of associations—and their thinking, unlike the episodic and linear thought of the story writer, is kaleidescopic, concentric.

*

How, then, to write the narrative poem? Best to find an action that may be explored in a variety of ways as it unfolds, so that what happens in the poem has the sense of being simultaneous, as in, say, Rich's "Diving into the Wreck," or Bishop's "The Moose." Best to combine the narrative and the lyric.

*

Elizabeth Bishop, while still a student at Vassar and trying to find a way to describe the poetry she writes and wants to write, says in a letter there are two kinds of poems—those "at rest" and "in action"—and adds that she favors the latter kind. To explain what she means by "action," she refers in this instructive passage to her models, the writers of baroque prose: "Their purpose was to portray, not a thought, but a mind thinking. . . . They knew that an idea separated from the act of experiencing it is not the idea that was experienced. The ardor of its conception in the mind is a necessary part of its truth."

*

How different Elizabeth Bishop is from the poet who must work for a living. I teach and then return home to grade papers. Bishop writes a letter to say she's thinking of buying a clavicord—then buys one, taking lessons on it because she feels this will help her poetry.

*

How does one respond to the maddening complaint of students that poetry which touches on sorrow is "depressing," when it is clear they speak for the American culture that made them?

I am told that a Russian does not, like the American, say "Fine" when asked how he is. He uses the time-honored gesture of the hand that says "So-so" or "It could be worse." The response suggests an awareness of life's difficulties, which we as human beings know well, wherever we may live. It does not insist on happy endings or the need to provide them; it suggests that things do not always come out well, that life includes not only affirmation but tragedy. It is not mythic; it is realistic.

Can anyone deny how dangerous our compulsion to affirm is to the affairs of the nation? Unable to address our complex social problems—the widening gap between rich and poor, the racial troubles, the murderous acceleration of American life—with a confident smile, we tend to deny them, insisting that "we're number one" in the great country of happy outcomes, whether that country exists or not.

The student who finds poetry that is grim or sorrowful "depressing" must be shown the impoverishment of his American mythology—perhaps by introducing him to his own national tradition in literature, including novelists from Melville to Faulkner, playwrights from O'Neill to Williams, and poets from Dickinson to Rich—developing early and late a tragic vision that might mature the nation.

Or show the student through his writing itself—how his truest work comes from dealing with the flawed world as he really knows it, beyond the cliches of American happiness.

*

"I tell my fiction students if anyone says or does something I can use in a story, it's mine, with no apologies," says Sharon Sheehe Stark, and she's right to tell them so. We are all obligated to give our stories and our poems what they need to live. One must decide whether one wants to be polite or to be a writer.

*

Here is Galway Kinnell seated among students, yet several states and countries away from them, in his own time zone, as he observes the young man asking the question. In his own time, from his own time zone, he responds.

In the car on the way up from the airport he is closer, though still, and I sense always, apart. We have a lively conversation about the tired syntax of contemporary American poetry—that generic sentence that begins with a declarative and follows up with qualifiers, often participial phrases or verb complements or objects in a series, direct or prepositional. We agree that Dickinson and Frost offer fine models of the delayed verb, and of a less predictable syntax in general.

As we near my house at the end of our trip, Kinnell speaks of his search for a way to refer to Frost at his upcoming investiture as Vermont's Poet Laureate, and I suggest he read Frost's short poem, "On Being Chosen Poet of Vermont," which he does not know. Standing in my kitchen to read the poem for the first time out of my Frost *Collected*, he nods and smiles, in the time zone of his delight.

*

Galway Kinnell does as Frost used to do: delivers his poems from memory. Patricia Smith does the same, insisting that when poets address their audiences directly, saying their poems and not reading them, they make a stronger impact. Yet the page has its value as a prop. In moving his eyes from page to audience and back again, the poet is demonstrating that his reading is about more than the exchange between him and the audience—that the reading also has to do with words written down as a private act, now being made public, an act that requires time and care and love.

*

An essay seeks to tell. A poem seeks to, in Frost's words, "tell how it can," all emphasis on the "how." An essayist must get to the point; the poet must avoid getting to the point, leaving the point to the reader. The essay is a statement; the poem is a riddle.

*

Except that essays are often poetic, and poems, essay-like. Though the prevailing aesthetic insists that poems should show rather than tell and above all avoid the didactic, we have the poetry of Jeffers, Whitman and the Psalms to prove that poems may also declare and instruct. We poets must be careful, given our obligation to pass on to our fellow humans whatever vision we have, not to let the prevailing aesthetic take our voices away and reduce our poetry to fragments.

*

At the academic gathering, I relearn that the academic most wants to take things apart; I, on the other hand, want to put things together—prefer my frog alive rather than dissected. In presentation after presentation, we are proudly offered pieces of the frog. Applause follows. Nobody mentions the stink.

*

In the creative writing class as it is too often taught, the instructor abdicates his role as authority and guide, either because he does not know how to say what works in student writing, or because he doesn't have the will to deal with student egos. The subject shifts from what is effective and what isn't to what feelings the author had when writing it, and what similar feelings the class can "share." Sharing by all members, including the abdicating professor, is at a premium, as it is in the counseling group, this class's true model. And in an age when personal feeling and sincerity make us all, from movie star to president, authentic, the students take it for granted they're doing real work.

*

In a letter John Keats likens the schoolroom to life's circumstances, adding that the hornbook of the schoolroom is the heart—and that learning to read that hornbook, we develop our souls. This was before the schoolroom came to be known by poets as the workshop.

*

During the afternoon before his reading on campus, I try this proposition on William Stafford: that American poets today tend to work on the model of the creative writing seminar, conducting workshops through the mail by sending their poems to poet friends who send the poems back with suggested revisions. Check the acknowledgments page of the standard collection today, I tell him, and you'll find who the seminar members are, adding that my friend Jane Kenyon jokingly calls her group "The Committee."

The whole idea flabbergasts Stafford. "Not even my wife makes suggestions about my work," he says. Later on, he comes back to the subject, asking what other "committees" I know of, and who is on my own committee. By the end of his visit The Committee has taken on a Bolshevik connotation, the sense of an institution out to subvert and control poetry itself. When I defend what seems to me the reasonable practice of testing new work out on friends, Stafford only replies, "We live in an occupied country."

Stafford repeats the remark when the name of a certain well-known poet and judge of poetry contests comes up in our conversation. He likens the poet-judge to a fish inspector expert in determining which fish should be kept as they pass before him and which should be tossed aside. The trouble is, he adds, that something might pass that's well worth keeping, just isn't a fish.

*

Straightforward in his response to The Committee, Stafford is more often, like his poems themselves, oblique. In the two-and-a-half days I host him between Maine readings, he seldom answers a question directly, preferring indirection; so he responds with another question, or with an anecdote (like his story about the fish inspector), or by quoting what someone else once said when asked a question similar to my own. Critics liken Stafford to Frost, meaning he also writes "popular" poetry. I'd liken him to Frost in the conditional way he writes and talks, never quite telling you where he stands, or all he means.

*

Someone once remarked that what drives every piece of writing is a question. The difficulty for the poet is how not quite to answer the question, placing it in the consciousness of the reader.

*

Poetry is the art of disclosure. As the poem moves, it must not only reveal but conceal, saving itself for its final unfolding, which must also give the sense of things withheld. In this process, the timing of image and awareness is essential. Nothing must be disclosed too soon or too late.

*

The poem must have something fast and something slow.

*

The new approach is what American magazines and providers of poetry fellowships often seem to be after, looking for evidence of a new mind. Yet poetry is after ancient things: the experience of the five senses, the link between the mind and the heart. To know poetry, we need to put aside the American mythology of newness, together with the emphasis on the mind as separate from the body and its intuitive life.

*

In an age when awards for achievement are handed out to new writers left and right, it is important to remember that the writer of true work builds slowly. He will be lucky if one day, long after the awards are handed out, a certain mist clears, and observers notice a building all intact, where there had not been one before.

*

The question in this period when poets make the university their home is how not to let the academy put its stamp on them. The best college is the one that allows the poet to think of himself as a writer more than a professor, to walk freely in the world.

*

Though his small size may make us overlook him, the rat, Emily Dickinson shows in poem #1356, has great power precisely *because* he is "concise" and "reticent," and so he can set up housekeeping wherever he wants without the need to pay rent, having his thoughts—his "schemes"—all to himself. Dickinson's rat is of course a version of herself, the poet who made her writing life apart from the literary establishment through concise and reticent and very powerful poems. The rat also reminds me of Linda Pastan, whose poems I read in quantity before hosting her in our visiting writers series. Given the noise and the big gestures of her generation of American poets, you might not notice her at first, off by herself, intent on the schemes of her verse. And then you discover what she's written—poems which, though they may lack Dickinson's range of language and grammar, are similarly small, with their own power to overwhelm.

*

The novelist is a carpenter. His gift is seen in the dimensions of his creation. To appreciate what he has done, we must stand back. The poet is a jeweler, whose gift is in smallness. To appreciate his creation, the work of a magnified eye, we must look closely.

*

The process of poems is braille-like, allowing the reader entry by touch, so that what forms in the mind and heart forms first in the hand. In writing a poem, we must find the right thing—familiar and yet mysterious to the touch—to place in the reader's hand.

*

Philip Levine does not shake your hand so much as press it, as if to place a token in it, something between the two of you that you may take away and later on, ponder the meaning of. Straightforward and even blunt in his speech, he is at the same time tender and interior. It is a manner I come to associate with the poems from *What Work Is,* which he reads from during his visit here—poems that are direct, just as the poems of *Not This Pig* were, but that replace the muscular assertion of his earlier work with a tone that is delicate and interrogative.

How deep in Levine is the narrative impulse! He himself speaks about it on the way to a discussion with students, drawing a contrast between himself and Charles Wright, who was astonished to discover the older poet "thought in stories" since he, Wright, didn't even dream in stories. I start the discussion by asking Levine if he has any advice for student writers, and he begins a long narrative about his development as a writer and poet at Wayne University in Detroit and afterward, finishing by summarizing the story's lessons. Levine's storytelling includes dirty jokes, one of which he tells me at our final lunch with the timing of a master.

*

Besides what I must have learned about storytelling from the dirty jokes I first told as an adolescent—the arrangement of details, the timing of the narration—I learned, I see now, how to "speak American" from them. There is a vernacular roughness in the telling that embodies the age-old American irreverence toward polite society. Also, since dirty jokes are meant to be shared apart from polite society, there's a subversiveness in the language, and a delight in the subversiveness. Yet there's a delicacy, too, a way the teller must have of taking the reader into his confidence for the private moment in which the joke is shared. All of these ways of speaking are helpful in the creation of an American voice.

The dirty joke also gave me and I'm sure many others the first exposure to surrealism: the man who had his penis lengthened by the addition of a baby elephant's trunk, and was embarrassed at the cocktail party when the hostess passed out peanuts. After such jokes, Magritte seems tame.

*

So here is Randy the small engines man trying to tell me how to troubleshoot my failed lawn tractor over the phone. Never mind that the steps he gives are hard to follow and even out of order. Listen to the accent and rhythm of his speech, rehearsed for this conversation all his life; here is the true order, in which there is not one mistake. Forget how he is supposed to say it and listen to how he says it.

*

Lore Segal, on our campus as a Woodrow Wilson Writing Fellow, tells me about her graduate student who writes in forms and claims that free verse has no tradition—that its line breaks, which have replaced rhyme, are merely arbitrary. Yet free verse's tradition is older than the tradition of rhyme and meter, going back to the beginnings of earnest human conversation. When we speak to someone we care about on a subject that matters to us, we all use line breaks; thinking and feeling the sentence, as one does in free verse, requires it. In fact, when we hear someone who does not speak in line breaks or does so in a programmatic way, we know we are listening to a commercial or a political speech, and we suspect lying. So the line breaks of spoken language also have to do—as does poetry—with telling the truth.

Shaping the free verse poem, then, we imitate the process of thoughtful and truthful conversation, our line-breaks indicating the stresses of our meditation as we say our sentences.

*

What is in that space the sentence of the free verse poem takes into itself as it goes down the page from line to line, becoming more poetic as it moves? It is a wordlessness which the lines touch against and make expressive, claiming it, too, as part of the poem. It is also the image of thought itself as it snaps from one line to the next, so as the poem moves we glimpse at the edge of the right margin the mind at work making the poem.

*

My friend Maxine Kumin, a witty concluder of poems, writes that a poem's ending should be definitive, like the click of the bolt in the doorjamb. Still, I prefer my door just ajar.

*

It was Philip Booth, if memory serves, who wrote in a poem published sometime after the moon landing in 1969 that Americans should "come to your senses." In the electronic nineties, as we continue to deify technological advances and the mechanical understanding they represent, Booth's words should appear on banners in every city and town. Now as always, the true knowledge is the knowledge of the heart, and true human advancement results from events as small as the lightness a poet might feel on discovering a new way of thinking and feeling. No one will ever televise such an event, nor will it deposit a man on the moon. But it may help us to come to our senses.

*

Reading Gerald Stern's *Selected Poems* before his appearance on campus, I find those few beautifully complete poems on which his reputation mainly rests. Most of them are about animals victimized by technology, through which he reflects on the affliction of our own animal selves, so dominated by the civilization we have made that we can't hear their cries. Of these poems, "The Dog" is the most wonderful. Then there are his poems about the city, which reveal again the suffering of the deeper self (the instinctual, intuitive, sniffing, howling core of us), overwhelmed by the technology of the metropolis. Oh, the blasted cityscapes of Stern, their sorrow!

*

I spend time with Charles Simic before my reading for graduate students at the University of New Hampshire and rediscover his splendid humor, the humor of the damned, delivered out of the side of his mouth in a way that reminds me of the gangsters of old movies or the thugs of old comics. It says we are all in on the joke of Truth and Justice, and happy as a result to be outlaws in a club of outlaws. In his company I am a thug poet, pleased to be in the gang whose boss is Simic, and whose truth is poetry.

*

During his campus visit, Thomas Lynch muses about how difficult it must be for the loved ones of poets, who seek our attention about any urgent thing only to find us looking at something just over their shoulders.

*

"Unconscious," my fifth and sixth-grade teachers called me, and the two of them once fell into step behind me as I walked home for lunch to taunt me with the word. At home, my mother named me "Stubborn." Yet it was only by being both of these things that I became a poet.

*

A friend asks, partly in fun, If you could change something that happened in your life, what would it be? It occurs to me to say, surprising even myself with my seriousness, that because my life has given me the only materials I have as a poet, my objective must not be to change my life, but to accept it exactly as I have lived it.

*

Yet accepting what his life has brought is difficult for Donald Hall. I sit with him three months after Jane Kenyon's death at a memorial reading for her in the Frost barn in Derry, New Hampshire. As others read her poems, he sometimes makes comments to himself as if no one else were there: "Ah, Gus!" he says aloud, listening to her description of their dog. At the end of the event, he stands and tells the audience about the volume he and Jane worked on from February until her death—the book called *Otherwise*. Then, in this period he calls "the long day of three months," he takes up the manuscript of that book to read the new poems, his voice unsteady on the occasional passage that refers to him. Reading from that black notebook, his hair uncut and tangled, his feelings tangled too, he sustains himself for one more hour, the two of them still together in poetry.

*

The intuitive, feeling self is dangerous because it insists that we live real lives. So people will try to kill it with alcohol, overwork, or excessive church-going—there are lots of ways to do the job. Because poetry asks us to be connected with our feeling selves and be whole, against every impulse to compartmentalize and deny, it too is dangerous.

*

The wholeness poetry seeks is also dangerous to the classroom as we seem to have it—a place that defines intelligence according to the ability to rehearse and perform left-brain skills, like the sad schoolroom Philip Levine describes in his poem "Milkweed," where students experience

> the long day
> after day of the History of History

      or the tables of numbers and order
    as the clock slowly [pays] out the moments.

Given his education in such a place, it's no wonder that at the conclusion of this poem Levine's narrator ends up walking "the empty woods, bent over,/ crunching through oak leaves." But then "a froth of seeds" from a milkweed drifts by, engaging his memory and his heart, reminding him of the childhood world he knew before school stamped the life out of it. The difficult and subversive challenge for teachers of poetry and poetry writing is to find a spot indoors, among numbers, order and the clock, where such seeds might grow.

The Forest and the Trees
FOUR SEASONS FROM A JOURNAL ABOUT PLACE AND POETRY

According to the country saying, a fool is a person who can't see the forest for the trees. Yet there are other fools, and more of them, who can't see the trees for the forest. Exploring small things and the larger meanings they suggest, poetry teaches us to see both.

*

And how often trees and woods have been *seen* in the verse of New England, past to present, the trunks and leaves of elms, chestnuts, and birches inspiring poems by Anne Bradstreet, Henry Wadsworth Longfellow, and Robert Frost. Reading these poems one discovers, beyond the technological changes of the motor car, radio and TV, and the computer, the old spell cast by this place—and the continuity of our poetry.

*

All spring the tree that inspires me most is the dead elm my dogs and I pass on our daily walk. It is so tall not even the vines that climb its sides each spring can reach its highest branches; yet they go as high as they're able, decorating it with a lovely, green lace. From the castoffs of weed and decay, this surprising elegance.

*

Under the locust beside our driveway in Mercer, Maine, this June, another unexpected sight: Clyde Henderson & Son, electricians, turn up a day early to reinstall electric heaters on our first floor, bringing their country talk with them. The senior, asked how he is today, responds, "I been better, but it cost more." The junior, asked how complicated the job will be, answers, "It might take a few swear words."

*

Listen to northern New Englanders explain the location of a house, gravel pit or pond, and you will eventually hear the expression "over in there," or "down in there," as in: "Stay on the main road until you come to a general store on the left, then take your next right. Their summer camp is *down in there*." Thus does the landscape of forests, hills and hollows make its way into native speech.

*

Kinnell, Oliver, and Kumin have all written poems about picking and eating wild blackberries in a New England August, but no one has written of the leisurely talk which goes on in the blackberry patch and is partly why one goes there, taking a family member or friend along for the purpose. "Good pickin'," somebody says far off in the patch, and "They're loaded today." Nearer by, a woman tells of all the quarts she put up last year, and her companion tells about the blackberry cobbler she will make for her grown son. Then they recall picking, good and bad, in other patches and other seasons. Hearing such voices as they drift across the bushes, one could be in heaven—God, listening to each innocent reflection, and to each affectionate joke: the man's voice asking his wife stuck in the briars, "Who's winnin'—you or the thorns?"; the woman threatening to bake him a "green pie."

*

The sentence spoken between intimates in a thoughtful and leisurely conversation is a long and open sentence, hitched together by conjunctions like "but," "when" and "because," and punctuated by small hesitations, as they think which way the sentence should go next. If one were to write this sentence out, breaking lines where the hesitations occur, free verse poets might have a lively model for sentence-making in this period when poetic syntax is so often literary and dull.

*

September. The leaves in the surrounding forest begin to turn, and the ache inside comes back, that yearning for more of it, for fall to tear one open with its fierce oranges and blood reds, to carry one off in October winds, and November rains.

*

On a frozen weekend in February, William Stafford stays with me and my wife Diane between readings, bringing great warmth to our house. After he leaves I find this poem on his pillow, left as a gift—a poem another poet might have saved for publication, though for Stafford, the pleasure the poem would give us was publication enough.

McNair's Place

Because it is Maine, snow still lingers
till its own good time in reticent places
or turns its face in shadow away,
and any farm stays only partly yours,
retaining its Indian posture, no matter what
        century it is.
Even towns have a habit of straggling off
rough at the edges and allowing old barns
to hang around leaning along Main Street
reminiscing with stands of woodbine and
        popple and wild grape.
What sheriff could arrest a land like this
when the red stars come out to patrol the dark?
Snow backs off, streetlights hold still;
out there in a surge of trees, galloping

hills escape all the time where our country belongs to the world and knows no law, no owner, no state.

*

During her winter reading on my campus, Lucille Clifton reads her well-known poem "Homage to My Hips," which concludes with the lines, "I have known them/ to put a spell on a man and/ spin him like a top!" As soon as she reads them, her large audience claps and laughs—except for my friend Bill Roorbach, who often delays his laughter until he has fully assimilated a joke, and does so on this occasion, starting to laugh after everyone else has stopped. Without missing a beat, Clifton points in Roorbach's direction declaring, "That one's still spinnin'!"

*

"Nature's first green is gold," says Robert Frost, referring, perhaps, to that yellow fuzz one sees in trees that are just budding and leafing out in the springtime of northern New England after a long winter. Yet for the maple tree, the first green is brown—a russet which, one discovers on closer view, belongs to tiny leaves in the exact shape they will always have, astonishing as a baby's hand. Without the brown of maples in the forest, we would not see the yellow of birch and poplar half so well. Their brown sets the contrast that makes visible not only nature's gold, but the whole spectrum of early green in the trees coming back to life each May in northern New England.

*

Back in the mid-sixties at the Richards Free Library in Newport, New Hampshire, my birthplace, the poet Raymond Holden gave a talk about Frost, who had won the library's first Sarah Josepha Hale medal some years earlier. Holden's presentation, which I attended, inspired by the Thompson biography of Frost then out in its first volume, exposed Frost's darker side. Holden recalled his own experiences with the deceased poet's deception, speculated on the possibility of Frost's womanizing, and even quoted a parody Frost once wrote of Sarah Josepha Hale's famous poem, "Mary Had a Little Lamb":

> Mary had a little lamb;
> Its name was Jesus Christ.
> God, not Joseph, was the ram,
> But Joseph acted nice.

*

A Mercer neighbor, Denis Culley, tells me about a horse—his old work horse and friend, Dick. For some time now, the old-timers in our town have been advising him to get Dick a mate. "A horse gets lonely without one," they all say. Unable to afford another horse, Denis now goes out to the pasture on spring and summer nights after the work is done to stand quietly beside his horse. Of all the love stories I've ever heard, this is one of the most moving.

*

How beautiful is the texture of talk on summer nights when we sit with friends on porches or, as I did last night, on the back lawn in deck chairs under the trees. Its intimacy and directness reminds me of James Carse's description of talk in *The Silence of God*, "To speak from your heart is to receive the listener into your heart." One often hears that the modern age has abandoned poetry; yet communicating in this way, we are almost speaking poetry. How, then, have we abandoned it?

*

Stephen Bien, my general practitioner in Farmington, confides in me that one of the most wonderful things he does during his work day is the most common: listening to people's hearts—each one with its own beat, each carrying on by its own mysterious power.

*

The poet does not believe in miracles, but in mysteries.

*

According to Bei Dao, the Chinese poet and dissident, it is important for any poet to have a small group with whom he can share his secrets. So saying, he suggests a definition of poetry as a code which, shared with others, gives special knowledge and power to the sharers and the poet alike. It is a definition shaped by his life under political oppression, and it reminds us of the capacity poetry has to change us and our world.

*

Writing poetry is in its way a public act, done with an audience in mind. But it is also profoundly private, a process requiring long periods of silence during which the poet struggles with memories and hurts and wishes only he knows. The poet is insulated in his privacy by the slowness of his publication: some of the poems he writes will reach a magazine eventually, but only those poems the editor chooses, when he or she chooses to print them. Years will likely pass before the magazine poems are collected in a book, and years more before the book, hardly a priority in marketing, has reached all of its readers. By then, the poet will be well into other work—may have published another book, whose poems his audience will not find until later on. Thus, the poet is mostly alone with his work, distanced from his readers, and in a way that may finally be important to his development, also protected from them.

*

Most writers lead two lives. In one life, they are social creatures who work with others at tasks which, day in and day out, they complete. In the other, they are antisocial, working alone on tasks they do over and over and seldom finish. The first helps them to appreciate the second—also to bear its hardships.

*

In the middle of a long fall semester spent on tasks and sociability at the workplace, I edge toward a familiar despair— the knowledge that without the second life, the first would be all hardship, and difficult to bear.

*

Besides, the second life, for all of its trials, teaches us through the process of revision that obstacles beget opportunities, and that lasting things happen little by little. It also shows the importance of faith, which Charles Simic calls "the only principle of technique I know."

*

Two or three years ago I became reacquainted with an aging couple I met as a child in the first New England place I can remember: a project called Southview outside of Springfield, Vermont, where I lived with my impoverished, angry mother and my two brothers after my father left. Today, I receive a videotape of the couple's fiftieth anniversary celebration and play it on my VCR. Now and again on the tape, among the people who chat over cocktails or gather at a salad bar or show off their children, I recognize the two of them; then I find each of their daughters, my old playmates, now parents themselves. But the person I am most interested in is the one who appears in a slide presentation of the couple's years in Southview: myself as a child of seven or eight, sitting outside their apartment on a cold day with my younger brother and their three girls. The daughter who runs the slide-show points me out to the audience. "This boy grew up to be a poet," she says. There is a hum. Looking at him, the jacketless kid with a hole in his T-shirt, I also feel disbelief. And then, for the longest time, pleasure.

*

Those who have caused us early pain and loneliness, the sources of our art: should we detest them or kiss their feet?

*

Twice this week I hear the maxim that there are only two themes for writers, sex and death, and I remember Sharon Olds repeating it years ago at a poetry reading. Yet there is a third theme that is even more important: birth. For why do we write at all if not to create something new, and to bring new awareness to the mind and the heart?

*

Trees again. On a November drive shortly after moving from New Hampshire to Maine several autumns ago, my homesick wife Diane began to cry about the "friends" that had been taken from her. When she dried her eyes and I got her to talk about her grief, I discovered it wasn't people she meant, but the great, old maples that had stood at the edges of our property and our lives for fifteen years.

*

On CNN's "Headline News," of all places, a Buddhist turns up to speak about suffering, and then gratitude. Gratitude is rare among Americans, he says, because in a capitalist culture, people are conditioned to want and get, so receiving is what is supposed to happen. In fact, we are never fully satisfied with what we receive and only want more. Unable to know gratitude, the Buddhist explains, we remain spiritually childish.

*

But gratitude exists. This January, from the front window of our house in Maine, Diane and I watch snow coming to rest on the distant trees around our property, which seem suddenly enormous, as if the snowfall had made them grow. One has a low branch with twists in it like a dozen elbows. Another has three small branches that open at the very top, making a tiny tree. Our new friends.

*

Another spring, and I have just read Philip Booth's musings about the cost of "whatever trees were felled" for catalogs that come in the mail from the retailers. I, too, am troubled by this. Yet I am troubled by the combination of hurt and resignation I see in the face of Clayton Brann when he tells me during his annual spring delivery of firewood to my house that the recession has stopped the production of catalogs and newspaper inserts. Clayton is a simple and un-schooled man who would have difficulty replacing his work in the woods. "You wouldn't think a little thing like that could affect a man's living," he says. "But it does."

*

Driving in New Mexico as Diane and I do in late April and early May, the ridges of hills or buttes in the distance, we come upon poor rural towns not so different from the ones we know in Northern New England. But strewn across open, tree-less spaces far outside of any city, these settlements have a forlorn quality the New England towns don't have, impover-ished as they can be. There's a forlornness, too, in the com-mercial strip we pass outside of Santa Fe—Dairy Queens, McDonald's and real estate offices that look so puny and irrelevant against the dark, wild mountains. One wonders, was this all we humans could come up with in our covenant with such nature?

*

Traveling to other places we learn most about the places we leave behind. In the late 70s on a Fulbright, my family and I lived in the so-called Developing World of South America, discovering through a leaking faucet how little control we had over our daily life there. Trying to get the faucet fixed, I called a plumber, who never came. Then I decided to do the job myself, going to the neighborhood hardware store, which carried no washers—only wastebaskets, flashlights, saws, and nails. Taking the bus to other hardware stores, I found wash-ers, but none in the correct size. At last I caught on: it would be nearly impossible to fix this faucet. Thus I learned to spend my time on other things. On the other hand, the typical American living in the United States becomes so enticed by the illusion of control, he may not see through it for years. This is the place, after all, where fixing faucets and any number of other things is comparatively easy. One discovers each day more projects that need to be done until at last one has no time for anything other than fixing and doing. Surely our country is in its own way underdeveloped.

*

I watch a group of businessmen at the local McDonald's on a July afternoon and guess the content of their conversation—having to do with poor management at the workplace—by following their gesticulations. Flipping a hand open with a little bounce indicates how obvious proper methods ought to be; elaborately counting the fingers of one hand with the other indicates basics that have been overlooked; raising one finger and an eyebrow at the same time says, "This is the real point." Each participant must demonstrate he's been around this track before; each must be relaxed in his authority.

*

Efficient as any other American industry, the literary industry in our country presents to writers a range of slots. There are slots on the state and national levels for rising women novelists; nature or place writers in mid-career; senior female poets; junior "creative nonfiction" writers; ethnic or gay poets, male and female, young and old; and so on. Sometimes the slots are filled by worthy writers. But far be it for a slot to say, one way or the other.

*

Place is not only a noun but a verb; one cannot come to know it without locating oneself in it, a slow and interior process. Looking out my window in one more October as I write this, I see blowing and falling leaves whose altered color is so familiar I have not looked closely at them until now. They are part of me, together with the damp chill from last night's rain I experience though I am indoors, all carrying a feeling that belongs to this season and no other. What have I learned that I didn't know I knew from autumn—its bright warmth against the cold, its whirling change against the skeletons of trees— what but that the world is two things at once: a surface and an underneath, a source of celebration and of sorrow, a yearning and a giving in, life that goes on and death that takes it away.

*

The two-things-at-once of northern New England weather is on the mind of a man I meet at the post office in late October during a snowfall nobody predicted. "Nice weather we're havin,'" he remarks. The irony of his familiar jest, containing its own two-things-at-once, is characteristic of this region's humor, whether one hears it in the local store or the stand-up comedy of Tim Sample. Referring to irksome or calamitous events with an understated delivery, that irony suggests not only the world's unpredictability, but the need to defend oneself against it, to control it.

*

Speaking a language studiously derived from Yankee speech, Robert Frost made irony a central device, and it gave him his strength and limitation as a poet. For while his irony allows him control over unpredictable and possibly threatening situations, it also prevents the sort of understanding that can only come from a risky investigation. Frost's reflex of irony makes him step back even from the celebration of "Birches," perhaps his most affirmative poem. So after describing a perfect balance between heaven and earth through the act of swinging on a birch tree, he ends his poem with ironic understatement: "One could do worse than be a swinger of birches."

I have long admired the ambiguity Frost brings to poetry with words like if, seems, and though; still I am glad there

are poets who do not stand outside the situations they de-
scribe, but enter wholly into them.

*

I bring Hayden Carruth to my campus in November, and
at dinner beforehand, he proves to be taciturn—perhaps
because he is shy, and in part because he is uncomfortable
with the bid for approval that social talk often requires. An-
other visiting writer might feel compelled to fill the gaps in
our conversation. Carruth feels no such obligation. Yet he
does, in his way, engage with the rest of us, teasing an old
friend he's staying with, Mitch Goodman, about how
"yuppified" his house has become with its electric blankets,
and asking around the table which of us are academics.
"Good," he says when he discovers someone not connected
with the university, and he gets a great kick out of Goodman's
story of his younger days as a university fellow on the dole at
Harvard, eating resplendent meals in a room with "a moose's
head sticking out of the wall."

When the conversation turns to his reading and I men-
tion a photo sent by his publisher, I learn it is twelve years
old. There's a more recent one, Carruth tells me, that ap-
peared in the *New York Times* not long ago—a photo he doesn't
much like. "Now everybody in the world knows I look like a
bum," he jokes. Then, more seriously, this poet in his seven-
ties whose important work is only now being fully recognized
shrugs his shoulders and adds, "I never did get how to deal
with this publicity thing."

*

Joining New England poets going back to the beginning
of the region's poetry, Carruth writes again and again about
trees, nowhere more beautifully than in "The Way of the Con-
venticle of the Trees." He chooses this poem near the end of
his presentation at my college, describing the years he has
spent gazing at the "homely American faces" of trees. "I have
looked at them out the window/ So intently and persistently,"

he reads, "that always/ My who-am-I has gone out among them/ Where the fluttering ideas beckon." Listening to this moving encounter, hearing Carruth call each of the "dear ones" he has loved all his life by name, the audience responds with sustained applause; for they too have loved trees, without words like these to say so.

*

Is the sense of place about to become another American nostalgia, as Sven Birkerts fears—undone by the global economy, satellite TV, and the virtual places of the Internet? And if so, what fate for the sense of self and identity that place provides? I ask a fellow poet, Peter Harris, these questions, and he reminds me of how often our poems locate us in the particulars of here and now, preserving those places in language. So I come to understand that poetry is an antidote to the increasing placelessness and *dis*location of America—that by calling us away from distraction to inhabit their moments or occasions, poems encourage the very sort of awareness that the forces of contemporary life seem bent on leaving behind.

*

Like poetry, place shows us how particulars may lead to universals. Coming to know over time our location's weather and slant of light, its geography and seasons, the behavior and speech and character of its people, we gradually understand our place as metaphor, seeing it not only in terms of our own lives but life in general wherever it is lived. In the end, our place is a source of vision, teaching us about all places.

*

The trials of end-of-the-semester over and done, and the snow having settled long since on the fields and forests of central Maine, I enter the delicious, dark season of winter here with its sweet sense of being cut off from everybody, and from everything I have ever written, except this poem I now turn to in my notebook, this song I sing in my head.

*

As a winter wind blows outside, two other poets and I entertain ourselves by reciting the first poem we can remember. One responds with a short poem by an English poet I've never heard of; the other recites a poem by Poe. The verse I say, I learned from pre-school friends:

> Fat and Skinny
> Had a Race
> Up and Down
> The pillow case.
>
> Fatty said
> It wasn't fair,
> So Skinny pulled off
> His underwear.

I came into the world of poetry, it turns out, as a populist.

*

After revising a mere five-page piece of prose Lord knows how many times, I decide it is at last ready to show to a friend; I fold it into an envelope and mail it to him. Later, just before the mailman comes, I'm taking the envelope out, having discovered a bad phrasing I've somehow missed. The next day my revision of a revision goes into a new envelope, which I mail for real, convinced of its worthiness—then see, two days later, the need for a different sentence at the end of the piece: how could I have sent the essay with a mistake so obvious? I think anew of my friend's eyes meeting the offending passage. Let this account show how important perfection is to writers, aware more than most of the world's imperfection. Let it show also how they hope for approval, and how hard it is for them to accept it.

*

Yet today, making a copy of a particular letter a reporter from an area newspaper has asked to see, I find approval that warms me. At the top of the letter is an oval portrait of Sarah Josepha Hale, and the letter's text announces that I am to be this year's recipient of the Hale Medal, given over the years to New England poets I have long respected. The news pleases me all the more because I will receive the prize in the place of my birth, at the center of the rural life I once lived and went on to write about.

Diane reminds me of the night over thirty years ago when we lived in Newport and Richard Wilbur received his Hale Medal. A high-school teacher back then with an abundance of kids and little money, I couldn't afford the required admission fee, so we and a friend stood outside the hall and watched with great yearning as Richard Wilbur went inside with his red-haired wife and several others, dressed to the nines. This year, I will go inside with no need to pay a fee, my red-haired wife on my arm.

*

Being out of money and teaching are often linked, as many teachers know. From my early years at Colby-Sawyer College, in New Hampshire, this memory: I am in the president's office, showing him a chart that proves my salary is exactly $200 above the poverty level for a family of six. Yet I have written and published poems, I say, and even won a grant. He listens with an expression of presidential sympathy, then tells me how concerned he is, not only for faculty salaries, but for all of the budgetary priorities he must deal with. I leave, gradually understanding the meaning of what he has just told me: this is my problem. So I begin a discouraging schedule of additional instruction at nearby colleges, and learn a lesson that poets at more privileged universities sometimes discover too late: that the academy can do the poet harm. And when I continue to write poems in spite of how busy I am, I learn one more valuable lesson: how necessary poetry has become to me, like a hungry weed that finds the crack in the sidewalk.

*

Then there is the discouragement of the rural dog. This April the one across the road outside my study window barked for days at family relatives arriving in their cars, all paying their last respects to the old man dying of cancer. Nature itself seemed to respond to the event, the grass of the lawn around the house brown, the single tree budless. For her part, the dog kept up her noise until each visitor went indoors, then sat beside her chain in the little space where she has lived all her life, gazing longingly toward the windows. Finally the old man, as close to a master as she ever had, died without saying goodbye to her, and his wife, who has no use for dogs, began her daily ritual of setting its food down in the space and leaving without so much as a word. Today, the dog has found a small stick near her house. In a light rain, all by herself, she walks briskly back and forth with the stick in her mouth.

*

Another dog, a different sort of longing. Our terrier Annie sits in the front seat of the car as the grass and trees fly by with her head cocked this way and that at the air vent: her nose radio.

*

At my mother-in-law's house for the weekend, Annie sits the whole day by the door to the cellar, where the cat has been shut. Meanwhile, I sit across from my wife's cousin, who (though I do not laugh) is hilarious in the way she puts one large leg over the other one and exhales from her cigarette while uttering some familiar witticism about the person under discussion, like, "Rebel without a clue."

*

My mother-in-law spends the weekend in her recliner, beside her pills and cane. Raised on a farm in Benton, New Hampshire, she is the sole custodian in our family of old country mottos she has never forgotten and still uses, often with an ironic twinkle. For her young granddaughter who sings before eating in the morning: "Sing before breakfast, cry before night." For the teenage grandson who can't stay out of trouble: "He isn't over Fool's Hill yet." For her son-in-law who has expectations: "There's many a slip between the cup and the lip."

*

I meet with the literary committee in a less cheering setting—a trendy deli that serves lunches with foreign names to upscale white guys. Everyone sits around eating the new food: pockets containing feta cheese mixed with bits of cucumber and tomato, or small platefuls of lettuce with melon cubes and nuts. There isn't a french fry in sight.

*

Over nachos and salsa at our favorite bar, my friend Bob Kimber declares that a good writer "knows when to shut up"— understands, that is, the value of silences. Surely Kimber is right. By bringing us artfully to the edge of silence, a writer can make us aware of things he does not say, and moreover of things neither he nor we are able to say—the silence beyond human explanations.

*

At a June conference on the poetry of E. A. Robinson held in Gardiner, Maine, Robert Mezey refers to Robinson's obsession with meanings that don't quite make themselves evident to us. "This immanence of something that does not take place," he says, "is, perhaps, the aesthetic experience." Like the best teachers of poetry, Mezey explains it by touching on poetry himself.

*

The sun is just up, and outside the house light has entered the leaves of maple and oak. They shimmer in a continuous breeze. It is early summer, one of those cool mornings in the country that make one shiver with the sense of things about to happen.

*

August, the month of the three best tastes of summer, two from our garden and one wild: corn on the cob, fresh tomatoes, and blackberries. Today, having tasted the first two for a week now, I go to gather the taste of the third at my customary place for picking, Wilder Farm, in Norridgewock, Maine. The barbed shoots and broad leaves of wild blackberries have taken over the old tie-up beside the barn there. A huge patch has replaced the kitchen garden behind the house. This is my patch, the wilder of the two on Wilder Farm; pulling my long-sleeve shirt over my head to protect against the prickles, I'm already thinking of the berries that wait in secret places I know so well. I pre-weigh my pails under the kindly eye of Mrs. Wilder, an ancient, white-haired lady who always rounds the weight off in my favor. Then I take the cut-away plastic milk bottle and twine she hands me, tie the bottle to my belt, and walk the old path, past the goats who mutter down at me from the barn windows, past a free-ranging rooster and his hens, past a sunken Mercedes, to the rock at my entrance of choice. *My* entrance, *my* patch. So much of the whole experience, I have to admit, is about *mine*, most of all the heaping pails of berries I intend to take home with me and hoard in our freezer. Yet even as I fill the milk jug and dump it into my first pail, I think of a favorite poem about blackberrying that has nothing to do with hoarding. Appropriately titled "August," this verse by Mary Oliver introduces a blackberry patch "nobody owns" and a narrator who has no interest whatever in collecting her harvest. In fact, this narrator eats everything she picks—hungry not only for wild blackberries but for a connection with the wild itself, which she finds in the poem's conclusion:

> . . . In the dark
> creeks that run by there is
> this thick paw of my life darting among

the black bells, the leaves; there is
this happy tongue.

Though I don't eat the blackberries I pick, Oliver's tri-
umphant poem makes its impact. I fill my milk jug thinking
of the wild taste I will bring to my tongue in January.

*

And isn't picking berries in each new season also a way
of reconnecting with the past—all those times one visited the
wild places where they grew, going back to childhood? Thus
the peculiar character of my daydreaming whenever I gather
blackberries, remembering the Maxwell House coffee can I
once twined around my belt; the parents and brothers I picked
with, finding my own secluded spot; and the look of berries
being poured from small containers into larger ones at the
end of a long afternoon which—do I only imagine it?—seems
resolved and happy.

*

The place where I live, how wild *it* is. This weekend I fly
over it with a friend in his small airplane and find nothing
but forest all the way to the horizon; yet on the ground in my
Maine town I hardly notice the surrounding trees, they seem
so far from houses and roads. Now when I see deer entering
our fields or a moose stumbling across a sidestreet, I will un-
derstand they know my region as it really is: a continuous
underworld of green, opening into a dream of light.

*

After a fall morning spent among the trees in the forest
of poetry, I too stumble into the street, out to take my daily
walk. Everywhere, this strangeness of houses and people walk-
ing to their mailboxes or tending their gardens. Everywhere
this assumption that life is all here, out in the open.

*

As my dogs walking with raised ears and curious noses alongside me well know, my northern New England place *is* out in the open. Yet poets in the past and the present of this location—Dickinson, Robinson, Frost, Francis, Eberhart, Kenyon, Hall, Booth, Kumin, Carruth, Oliver, and all the rest—suggest that to discover one's place, one must travel not only in the world, but in the underworld of feeling and thought and memory. Through my writing, I take this second journey, gradually aware as I do so how being here contributes to being.

About the Author

The recipient of grants from the Rockefeller, Fulbright and Guggenheim foundations, Wesley McNair has held an NEH Fellowship in Literature, and two NEA Fellowships for Creative Writers. He has won the Eunice Tietjens Prize from *Poetry;* the Theodore Roethke Prize from *Poetry Northwest;* and the 1997 Sarah Josepha Hale Medal, among other honors. The editor of *The Quotable Moose: Contemporary Maine Writing,* he is the author of five books of poetry, the first of which, *The Faces of Americans in 1853,* was selected as a Classic Contemporary by Carnegie Mellon University Press. His two most recent volumes are *Fire* and *Talking in the Dark* (David R. Godine, Publisher). He is the director of the creative writing program at the University of Maine at Farmington and lives with his wife Diane in Mercer, Maine.